Put Your Life Together

Studies in the Book of Ruth

by Warren W. Wiersbe
General Director
Back to the Bible

A
BACK TO THE BIBLE
PUBLICATION
LINCOLN, NE. 68501

VICTOR
BOOKS a division of SP Publications, Inc.
WHEATON ILLINOIS 60187

Offices also in
Whitby, Ontario, Canada
Amersham-on-the-Hill, Bucks, England

55,000 printed to date—1985
(5-3517—55M—65)
ISBN 0-8474-6512-8

All Scripture quotations are from *The New Scofield Reference Bible.*

Printed in the United States of America

Contents

Chapter 1

Good News in Bad Times

A New York hotel maid walked into a room one day, intending to get it ready for the next occupant. Then she discovered that the former occupant had not yet departed. He was lying there dead, for he had committed suicide. The maid found this note: "I leave to society a bad example. I leave to my friends the memory of a misspent life. I leave to my father and mother all the sorrow they can bear in their old age. I leave to my wife a broken heart and to my children the name of a drunkard and a suicide. I leave to God a lost soul that has insulted His mercy."

Here was a man whose life had fallen apart because of sin. It's a shame that no one explained to him what Jesus Christ can do to put our lives back together again.

The Book of Ruth tells us about a family that fell apart, about a woman who became bitter toward God and about how God rescued this family and put their lives back together. You and I are involved in the Book of Ruth. Through Ruth, David came into the world, and through the family of David our

Saviour came into the world. If it were not for Ruth, we would have no Saviour!

A Look at History

The Book of Ruth begins, "Now it came to pass in the days when the judges ruled." The Book of Judges describes a time in history when Israel was in trouble. Everything in society was falling apart. Yet, in the midst of that period, we have this beautiful story about Ruth and Boaz—about their love for each other and about God's leading in their lives.

No King

The Book of Judges is the book of "no king": "In those days there was no king in Israel, but every man did that which was right in his own eyes" (Judg. 17:6; see also 18:1;19:1;21:25). When you read the Book of Judges, you discover it is characterized by anarchy, apostasy and apathy. The tribes of Israel were apathetic, for they failed to go up and take the land to claim it for their inheritance. They were indifferent to the Lord and His blessing. Their apathy led to apostasy; they compromised and lived like the heathen nations, which were characterized by idolatry and immorality. Their apostasy ended in anarchy with every person doing what was right in his own eyes.

We have a similar situation in society today. We are living in a period similar to the one in the Book of Judges, spiritually speaking. There is no king in Israel today, and people are doing what they please. Therefore, we have no peace in our world.

6

Man's King

First Samuel is the book of "man's king." The people of Samuel's day cried, "Give us a king that we might be like the other nations!" (see I Sam. 8). God gave them a king—Saul from the Tribe of Benjamin. Saul was never meant to be the king who would establish a dynasty in Israel. How do we know this? Because we are told very clearly in Genesis 49:10 that the king was to come from the Tribe of Judah and not from Benjamin. God gave them Saul to discipline them, to chasten them and to teach them some lessons. First Samuel is the book of "man's king." Saul began with great fervor and success, coming as a deliverer. But he closed his career as a destroyer. He began as a peacemaker, but he ended his life as a peace-breaker and a persecutor. Finally, he committed suicide.

I think Saul is a perfect illustration of the Antichrist. One of these days the world will be in such a mess that people will cry out for a ruler: "We must have a ruler! We must have someone to hold things together!" Satan will have his masterpiece all ready, and he will be "man's king." Like Saul, the Antichrist will come on the scene as a peacemaker and a protector, but he will become a peace-breaker and a persecutor. Finally, of course, the Antichrist will be destroyed by the coming of our Lord Jesus.

God's King

Second Samuel is the book of "God's king." Who was God's king? David was, and he was one of

7

Ruth's descendants. David was a man after God's own heart, and he is a beautiful picture of our Lord Jesus Christ. David was born in Bethlehem of the Tribe of Judah as was Jesus Christ. David was a shepherd, and our Lord Jesus said, "I am the good shepherd" (John 10:11). David was rejected by his people, so it was several years before he officially sat on his throne. The Lord was also rejected by His people, but one day He shall sit on the throne of David. David defeated the enemy Goliath on the battlefield, while Jesus defeated Satan in the wilderness. David was chosen to reign, but he had to wait for his coronation. Christ has been appointed as God's King, but He is waiting for His coronation. One day He shall be crowned and shall reign in victory!

So Judges is the book of "no king." That's where we are living right now. Every person is doing what is right in his own eyes. First Samuel is the book of "man's king." That's where the world is headed. People are going to cry out for a deliverer. Second Samuel is the book of "God's king." God will send His King to straighten things out and to establish the true Kingdom.

A Look at the Book

The Book of Ruth is a beautiful love story in the midst of apostasy and anarchy. Ruth is one of two books in the Old Testament dedicated to the story of a woman. The other, of course, is the Book of Esther. We can see several contrasts between the two books. In Ruth you have a Gentile who married

8

a Jew; in Esther you have a Jewess who married a Gentile. The Book of Ruth begins with a famine, while Esther begins with a feast. The Book of Ruth ends with the birth of a baby, a new beginning. The Book of Esther closes with the hanging of an enemy. Ruth tells the story of poverty in Bethlehem and how God did something about it. Esther is the story of riches in a king's court. But both Ruth and Esther played significant roles in the history of Israel because they each helped to preserve their nation. God enabled Ruth to be the ancestress of David, and He enabled Esther to protect the nation from destruction.

Weeping

The Book of Ruth contains four chapters. I'd like to give a title to each of these chapters. It might help us remember what the book is about. I would like to call Chapter 1 "Weeping." Throughout this chapter we see trouble and weeping. Naomi, her husband, Elimelech, and their two sons, Mahlon and Chilion, go to Moab where the three men die. Naomi is left childless, so she decides to go back home. Naomi and her daughters-in-law, Ruth and Orpah, weep as they consider parting.

Naomi tells Ruth and Orpah to go back to their own home, kisses them good-bye and sends them on their way. Orpah sheds tears of *despair*, turns around and goes back home. Naomi weeps because of *disappointment*. But Ruth sheds tears of *devotion*. Ruth clings to her mother-in-law and gives a marvelous statement of faith. She has come to trust in the true and the living God! Chapter 1 is a story of sorrow. Everything is falling apart, but there is still hope because of Ruth, who has put her faith in the living God. She tells Naomi, "Thy people shall be my people, and thy God, my God" (v. 16).

Working

I will entitle chapter 2 "Working." In chapter 2 we find Ruth serving in the field as a gleaner. She picks up the grain that the reapers drop as they gather the harvest. This is not a very lofty position, is it? But then Boaz comes to her aid and falls in love with her. From that point on everything starts to change, even though Ruth does not realize who Boaz is until she goes home and talks to her mother-in-law.

Waiting

I shall call chapter 3 "Waiting." Naomi tells Ruth to present herself to Boaz, the kinsman-redeemer. Boaz can redeem them, pay their debts and set them free. Ruth, in a great act of faith and love, goes to Boaz and lies at his feet. This act is the turning point in the book. You find her at the feet of Boaz when she is gleaning (2:10), but at that time she is thanking him for his generosity. She does not know who he is or what he can do for her. She simply realizes that he is providing food and protection for her. But in chapter 3 she knows who Boaz is. She lies at his feet, and he says to her, "Fear not; I will do to thee all that thou requirest" (v. 11).

Ruth goes back home and tells Naomi what Boaz said. Naomi replies, "Sit still, my daughter, until thou know how the matter will fall; for the man will not be in rest, until he have finished the thing this day" (v. 18). Boaz is a picture of Jesus Christ, who finishes what He starts. He is the Alpha and the Omega. He promises us that what He begins, He will complete.

Wedding

Chapter 1 is filled with *sorrow.* Chapter 2 contains an account of *service.* Chapter 3 is a beautiful picture of *submission.* Now we come to chapter 4, which I will entitle "Wedding." We go from waiting to wedding and from submission to *satisfaction!*

Boaz goes to the gate and publicly redeems the land that belonged to Elimelech. At the same time, he redeems Ruth and marries her! In chapter 4 Boaz does everything. All Ruth does is accept his work, because Boaz is her kinsman-redeemer.

So Boaz took Ruth as his wife. God blessed her so that she bore a son whom they named Obed. Obed was the father of Jesse, and Jesse was the father of David. The story has a happy ending. But, remember, if Ruth hadn't lain at the feet of the lord of the harvest, Boaz, who was the kinsman-redeemer, everything would have fallen apart.

The story of Ruth can be studied from many aspects. It certainly is a picture of Christ and the Church. It also is an example of God's gracious working in the lives of people. But as we study this book, we shall look at how God puts people's lives back together. Through faith in Jesus Christ and by submission to Him, you can experience the fullness of the life that Jesus promised.

My prayer is that, as we study the Book of Ruth, we will all learn how to put our lives together—that we will not allow sin, rebellion or bitterness to rob us of all that God has for us.

How do lives fall apart to begin with? We shall learn that in the next chapter.

Chapter 2

You Can't Run Away From Problems
(Ruth 1:1-5)

Two mighty forces are at work in the world today. One force is pulling everything apart, while the other force is seeking to put things back together again. Sin is the destroyer, but Jesus Christ is the builder.

So many people need to put their lives together today! Their lives and homes are being pulled apart, and their jobs are in jeopardy. For these people, everything seems to be crashing down around them. They are falling apart physically, mentally, socially, financially and, most of all, spiritually. In the Old Testament book of Ruth, we have a vivid account of two widows—one young and the other old—who were able to put their lives together and find happiness and fulfillment in the will of God.

In chapter 1 of Ruth, everything is falling apart. Naomi and her family made some mistakes. People today are making these same mistakes. Let me survey the first chapter for you, and then we will look at the first mistake that Naomi and her family made and the reasons behind it.

13

Ruth 1:1-5 reveals the family's first mistake. They were *trying to run away from their problems*. Bethlehem-judah was experiencing a famine. Naomi, her husband and two sons packed up and went to Moab to avoid the famine and other problems. But in Moab they only found more problems!

The second mistake that Naomi made was *trying to cover up her disobedience* (vv. 6-18). She tried to send her two daughters-in-law back home so they would not come to Bethlehem with her and be evidence that she had disobeyed God. First, she ran away from her problems, and then she tried to cover her sins and hide them.

The third mistake that Naomi made is found in verses 19 through 22. She *became bitter against God*. Ruth went back to Bethlehem with Naomi, but Naomi was a bitter woman. The name "Naomi" means "pleasant," but she was not at all pleasant! She said, "Call me not Naomi, call me Mara; for the Almighty hath dealt very bitterly with me" (v. 20). The name "Mara" means "bitter." It comes from the same word as myrrh, the bitter perfume that was used for embalming.

If you want to destroy your life, then make these same three mistakes: try to run away from your problems, try to cover up your disobedience, and become bitter against God. I guarantee that if you will take these three steps, your life will begin to fall apart.

"Now it came to pass in the days when the judges ruled, that there was a famine in the land. And a certain man of Bethlehem-judah went to sojourn in the country of Moab, he, and his wife, and his two sons. And the name of the man was Elimelech, and the name of his wife, Naomi, and the name of his two sons, Mahlon and Chilion, Ephrathites of Bethlehem-judah. And they came into the country of Moab, and continued there. And Elimelech, Naomi's husband, died; and she was left, and her two sons. And they took themselves wives of the women of Moab; the name of the one was Orpah, and the name of the other, Ruth; and they dwelt there about ten years. And Mahlon and Chilion died also, both of them; and the woman was bereft of her two sons and her husband" (vv. 1-5).

The scene is now set. A famine has come upon the people of Israel. Instead of trusting God to provide, this family chooses to pack up and go to Moab. They decide to run away from their problems rather than facing them.

Why do people try to run away from their problems? Let me suggest several possible reasons.

Living by Sight—Not by Faith

One reason why this family ran from their problems is because *they were living by sight and not by faith*. In comparing their life in Bethlehem with life in Moab, they made the mistake of only looking at the situation from a human point of view. When they looked at Bethlehem, they only saw hunger and pain, while Moab appeared to be the land of plenty.

From God's point of view, their decision was wrong. Moab was a heathen land, and the Moabites worshiped false gods. They were the enemies of

15

God and of Israel. God had said in Deuteronomy 23:3, "An Ammonite or Moabite shall not enter into the congregation of the Lord; even to their tenth generation shall they not enter into the congregation of the Lord forever."

The Ammonites and the Moabites were the descendants of Lot as the result of an act of incest (see Gen. 19:30-38). When Lot was delivered from Sodom, he and his daughters lived in a cave. His daughters made him drunk and then committed incest with him. The sons born to these women became the fathers of the nations of Ammon and Moab, and these nations became the enemies of the people of God. From God's point of view, Elimelech and his family were leaving home and going to reside with, and depend on, the enemy.

The name "Bethlehem" means "house of bread." Judah can be translated "praise," while Ephratah means "fruitful." Bethlehem was called Bethlehem-Ephratah. As this family looked at the "fruitful house of bread," they could only see famine and barrenness. The sound of complaining filled the land of "praise." Elimelech said to Naomi, "The wisest thing we can do is leave." If you are living by sight and not by faith, difficult situations look hopeless to you. Running away seems like the best solution.

Why didn't they just trust God? God had made it very clear in His Law that if His people obeyed Him, He would bless them. We are told in Deuteronomy 28 that famines were a discipline from God. God promised to send the harvest, the rain and the

16

sunshine—all that was needed—if His people would obey Him. Instead of running away, the people should have run to God, bowed down, confessed their sin and asked for His forgiveness.

When you start living by sight and not by faith, then you will start running away from your problems and sins instead of trusting God to help you overcome them. You will try to find an easy way out of a difficult situation.

Living for the Physical—Not the Spiritual

A second reason why people run away from their problems is because *they are living for the physical and not for the spiritual.* Some people may argue, "Well, these people had to live!" I would rather be hungry *in* the will of God than full and satisfied *out of* the will of God.

The first temptation that Satan presented to the Lord Jesus was a choice between the physical and the spiritual. Our Lord had just spent 40 days fasting in the wilderness, and He was hungry. Satan said to Him, in effect, "Since you are hungry, turn these stones into bread." If the Father in heaven would have said to His Son, "Turn the stones into bread," Jesus would have done it. But the Father had not given Him that commandment. Jesus answered, "Man shall not live by bread alone, but by every word that proceedeth out of the mouth of God" (Matt. 4:4). Jesus did not succumb to the temptation to put His needs before the will of God.

I've often heard people say, "Well, a person *has* to live." While it is true that we must live in the will of

17

God, it is not true that we must live—no matter what the cost. It is far better for us to be poor and hungry in the will of God than to have all the comforts of life apart from the will of God.

This was the mistake that Esau made. He despised his God-given birthright. Esau had been out in the field hunting and came home famished. Jacob was making some delicious stew, and Esau sold his birthright for a bowl of it. He put his physical desires before God's plan for his life.

When you begin putting the physical ahead of the spiritual, you start living to please yourself. You begin to think that the most important thing in life is to be comfortable, not to be conformable to the will of God. What if our Lord Jesus Christ had put the physical ahead of the spiritual? What if He had been more concerned about His own comfort and pleasure than about doing the will of God? Where would we be today?

Living for the World—Not the Lord

A third reason why people make the mistake of running from their problems is because *they are living for the world and not for the Lord.* The Word of God says, "Now it came to pass in the days when the judges ruled" (Ruth 1:1). We have already discovered that the Book of Judges is the book of "no king." At least four times in the Book of Judges we read: "There was no king in Israel" (17:6;18:1;19:1; 21:25). Twice we read: "In those days there was no king in Israel; every man did that which was right in his own eyes" (21:25; see also 17:6). Naomi and her

18

family were living in an era of anarchy. The popular argument was "Everyone is doing it! Why shouldn't we?" But the fact was that everyone was *not* doing it! Boaz did not go to Moab. He stayed where he was, and God later used him to rescue Naomi and Ruth.

When the situation became difficult in Bethlehem, Naomi and her family made three wrong decisions: (1) they decided to leave Bethlehem; (2) they decided to go to Moab; and (3) after Elimelech died, Naomi allowed her two sons to marry women from Moab. In Ezra 9:1 and Nehemiah 13:1 you find both Ezra and Nehemiah protesting against the Jews who had married women outside the nation of Israel.

The problem today is that people are conforming to the world with its rebellious atmosphere and attitudes. When you start running away from your problems, you are living for the world and not for the Lord. Your excuse becomes "Everybody is doing it!" And you start doing what is right in your own eyes.

Ignoring the Source of the Problem

A fourth reason why people run from their problems is that *they ignore the real source of their problem—their own heart.* When Naomi, Elimelech and their two sons went to Moab, *they took their problem with them.* What was their problem? The spiritual deterioration in their hearts. *They* were the problem. They were proud because they believed they could manipulate and manage their

19

own lives and do a better job of it than God was doing.

The source of every problem is *inside*, not outside. The heart of every problem is the problem in the heart. We blame circumstances, and we even blame God. But when you reach the root of the problem, *we* are the ones who are to blame. We doubt God and disobey His Word. We put the world and the flesh ahead of the will of God. We think we can run away. But the Word of God makes it clear that when you run away, you take your sinful heart right along with you. That's why you can't run away; that's why running away only causes the problems to increase. You may be in a new location and have a new situation, but you still have the same old heart. You will repeat the same old mistakes. Ralph Waldo Emerson used to say that a change in geography will never overcome a flaw in character.

Naomi and her family traveled the 50 miles from Bethlehem to Moab, and it was a trip that took them out of the will of God. They planned to sojourn in Moab just for a while, but they tarried there for ten years. Everything fell apart. The fruitful fields of Moab became a cemetery for Naomi's husband and her two sons. Instead of having hope, Naomi became hopeless. God had to discipline this family to bring Naomi back where she belonged. It never pays to rebel against God.

Unfortunately, Naomi still had not learned her lesson. We will see that she made another mistake. She tried to cover up her sins and blame other people. Hebrews 12:11 says, "No chastening for the present seemeth to be joyous, but grievous; nevertheless, afterward it yieldeth the peaceable fruit of righteousness unto them who are exercised by it." Naomi had to learn to surrender to the discipline of God and stop running away.

Chapter 3

You Can't Cover Your Sin
(Ruth 1:6-14)

The American poet Henry Wadsworth Longfellow wrote:

> Be still, sad heart, and cease repining;
> Behind the clouds is the sun still shining.
> Thy fate is the common fate of all.
> Into each life some rain must fall.

For the three widows in Moab, the storm of sorrow and trial was coming down in torrents. It wasn't just that "some rain" was falling. They were in the midst of a deluge! Naomi, Orpah and Ruth had to make some important decisions. God had disciplined Naomi for acting in unbelief by leaving Bethlehem and going to Moab. She had lost her husband and her two sons. What were these three widows going to do?

"Then she [Naomi] arose with her daughters-in-law, that she might return from the country of Moab; for she had heard in the country of Moab how the Lord had visited his people in giving them food. Wherefore, she went forth out of the place where she was, and her two daughters-in-law with her; and they went on the way to return unto the land of Judah. And Naomi said unto her two daughters-in-law, Go, return each to her mother's house; the Lord deal kindly with you, as ye have dealt with the dead, and with me. The Lord grant you that ye may find rest, each of you in the house of her husband. Then she kissed them; and they lifted up their voice, and wept. And they said unto her, Surely we will return with thee unto thy people.

"And Naomi said, Turn again, my daughters. Why will ye go with me? Are there yet any more sons in my womb, that they may be your husbands? Turn again, my daughters, go your way; for I am too old to have an husband. If I should say, I have hope; if I should have an husband also tonight, and should also bear sons, Would ye tarry for them till they were grown? Would ye refrain from marrying? Nay, my daughters; for it grieveth me much for your sakes that the hand of the Lord is gone out against me. And they lifted up their voice, and wept again; and Orpah kissed her mother-in-law, but Ruth clung to her" (Ruth 1:6-14).

When you find yourself in difficult circumstances because of God's discipline or because of someone else's disobedience, you can make one of three decisions. You can decide to *cover up*, which is what Naomi did; you can decide to *give up*, which is what Orpah did; or you can decide to *stand up* and believe God, which is what Ruth did.

23

Naomi Covers Up

Naomi decided to *cover up*. She made a right decision when she decided to go back to Bethlehem. She should have stayed there to begin with because Bethlehem was "the house of bread." Instead, she departed in unbelief and disobedience and went to Moab where the people were enemies of God. So she made a right decision to return to Bethlehem, the place of faith.

The victorious Christian life is a series of new beginnings. I have met people who try to convince me they are *always* on a mountaintop. But I've noticed that you cannot have mountaintops unless you also have valleys. We all have to make new beginnings, don't we?

Some of God's choicest people in the Bible had to go back. Abraham disobeyed God, left the land and went to Egypt. He had to return to the place where his altar was, and God forgave him. Jacob had to go back to Bethel. He had wandered far from God, and the Lord told him to go back to Bethel, the place where He had met him.

How can you be restored to fellowship? Go back to the place where you left the Lord. He didn't leave you—you left Him.

Naomi made a right decision to go back home, but her motive for returning was wrong. She was going, not to glorify the Lord but to obtain food. The Lord had given His people in Bethlehem food. She was still walking by sight, interested only in her physical well-being. She was still living for the physical and not for the spiritual. We have no evidence that she repented or confessed her sin. Instead, we find that she was bitter.

She had a wrong motive, and she used a wrong approach. She tried to get rid of her daughters-in-law. Naomi's advice to them used to perplex me. I could not understand why Naomi—a believer in the true God—would want to send her daughters-in-law back to Moab where they would be worshiping idols. I have come to the conclusion that she was trying to get rid of the evidence. If she brought Ruth and Orpah back to Bethlehem, they would be proof to her people that she had disobeyed the Lord. Not only had she gone to Moab, which was bad enough, but she had permitted her sons to marry the women of Moab. This, of course, was disobeying the Word of God. We read in the Law that the Jewish people were not to mingle with the other nations in the land. So she tried to get rid of Orpah and Ruth. She gave them bad advice and exerted a bad influence on them.

It is dangerous to listen to the advice of a backslidden believer. In fact, a backslidden believer can do more damage than an unsaved person. Naomi gave her daughters-in-law wrong counsel and tried to lead them back into their old life.

When you are facing difficult circumstances, you can try to cover up your sins as Naomi did. She said, "I'll go back home and start all over again, but I had better get rid of the evidence that I have been out of the will of God." The Bible says, "He that covereth

25

his sins shall not prosper, but whoso confesseth and forsaketh them shall have mercy" (Prov. 28:13).

Orpah Gives Up

When you are facing the difficult circumstances of life, you can *give up* as Orpah did. She started to go with Naomi to Bethlehem: "Then she [Naomi] arose with her daughters-in-law, that she might return from the country of Moab" (Ruth 1:6).

Naomi started for Bethlehem with both Ruth and Orpah accompanying her. They said to her, "Surely we will return with thee unto thy people" (v. 10). And yet she kissed them good-bye and encouraged them to go back to their people and to their gods (v. 15).

Orpah was a woman of indecision. She started to go with Naomi, she wept many tears, she kissed Naomi affectionately, and yet she turned around and returned to Moab. Naomi had appealed to Orpah's natural desires when she said, "Go back to your mother's house" (see v. 8). The word "mother" would certainly have touched Orpah's heart. Naomi said, "You ought to find rest in the house of your husband" (see v. 9). The word "husband" would also have meant something to this young widow. Naomi appealed to her sight, not to her faith. Naomi argued, "Look at me. I'm an old woman. I don't have any more children. I'm not going to have another husband. Even if I did get married right now, you wouldn't wait that long for my children to grow up" (see vv. 12,13).

So Naomi gave some very solid arguments as to

26

why Orpah should go back to her old life in Moab; she even blamed God. "Nay, my daughters; for it grieveth me much for your sakes that the hand of the Lord is gone out against me" (v. 13).

Orpah is a picture of people who are near to believing in the true God and yet are so far from it. She wept, she kissed her mother-in-law, she promised she would go along, and yet she went back to her idols, back to darkness.

You can get very close to the kingdom of God and still not enter in. It's possible for a person to show a great deal of emotion and determination and yet never do the will of God. Orpah, when she faced difficult choices, decided to give up. She said, "I'm going to go back where I came from."

The Book of Hebrews was written to tell us, "Don't go back! Keep going forward!" The Jews wanted to go back to Egypt, and God disciplined them because of their unbelief. When life became difficult, Orpah's faith wavered. Instead of trusting God to give her a new life, Orpah went back to her old life in Moab and was never heard of again.

Ruth Stands Up

The third choice you can make when faced with a difficult situation is to *stand up* as Ruth did. Ruth chose to remain with Naomi because she loved her deeply. When they arrived in Bethlehem, everyone soon heard about her love for Naomi. Boaz said, "It hath fully been shown me, all that thou hast done for thy mother-in-law" (Ruth 2:11). Everyone respected Ruth for her love and devotion to her mother-in-law.

27

They told Naomi that her daughter-in-law, who loved her, was better to her than seven sons (see 4:15).

Ruth stood up and declared her love for Naomi, but more than that, she gave a testimony of her love for, and faith in, God. Ruth said, "Entreat me not to leave thee, or to turn away from following after thee; for where thou goest, I will go; and where thou lodgest, I will lodge: thy people shall be my people, and thy God, my God" (1:16). Ruth was willing to go to a foreign country and live with strangers because of her faith in God and in Naomi. Later, Boaz said to Ruth, "The Lord recompense thy work, and a full reward be given thee by the Lord God of Israel, under whose wings thou art come to trust" (2:12). Ruth had put her faith in the true and living God, and she was sheltered under His wings.

When we are faced with difficulties in life, the only right decision to make is to stand up and trust God. Ruth made the right decision. It is really amazing that Ruth had any faith at all when we consider all the obstacles she had to overcome! She experienced more sorrow in a short period of time than most people could bear, for she saw the death of her father-in-law, her husband and her brother-in-law. Then Naomi complained about what God had done. In spite of the bad attitude of Naomi, the bad example of Orpah and her own natural tendencies to want to go home and be with her father and mother, this young widow still put her faith in the living God.

Ruth's testimony of faith is one of the greatest

confessions found anywhere in the Bible. I think it has a place alongside the great confession of faith that Peter made in Caesarea Philippi, when he declared that Jesus Christ was the Son of God. Ruth is an example to us all that you can trust the Lord, no matter what obstacles may be placed before you. You can declare your faith in the true and living God.

The one phrase that is repeated again and again in chapter 1 is "go back" or "return"—12 times to be exact. Ruth and Orpah were being pressured by Naomi to go back. Orpah yielded to the pressure and returned to Moab.

We are under that kind of pressure today. All the influences of the world and the flesh tell us, "Go back to your old life!" But God says to us, "No, don't go back. No matter how difficult the situation may be, no matter how fiercely the storm may be blowing, don't go back!"

Naomi made the wrong decision and tried to cover up her sin. Orpah made the wrong decision; she lost her faith, gave up and went back to her old life. But Ruth made the right decision. She chose to stand up and believe God.

You can make one of three choices when faced with a difficult situation because of your disobedience. You can blame God or someone else for your problems and try to cover up your sin; you can give up and return to your former, sinful life; or you can stand up, take responsibility for your actions, seek God's forgiveness and trust in Him.

When you live by faith, the future will look bright

and you can face it with confidence even in the midst of a storm. But when you depart from faith and live in unbelief and doubt, the future will always look hopeless to you. God will see you through if you will trust Him, if you will yield yourself to Him in faith.

> Trust and obey—
> For there's no other way
> To be happy in Jesus
> But to trust and obey.

Chapter 4

A Great Confession of Faith
(Ruth 1:15-22)

Orpah kissed Naomi and Ruth. She said good-bye to both of them, turned and headed back to her old life in Moab. Naomi tried to convince Ruth to follow her sister-in-law, but Ruth refused. Then Ruth gave one of the greatest declarations of faith found anywhere in the Word of God.

"And she [Naomi] said, Behold, thy sister-in-law is gone back unto her people, and unto her gods; return thou after thy sister-in-law. And Ruth said, Entreat me not to leave thee, or to turn away from following after thee; for where thou goest, I will go; and where thou lodgest, I will lodge: thy people shall be my people, and thy God, my God. Where thou diest, will I die, and there will I be buried; the Lord do so to me, and more also, if anything but death part thee and me. When she saw that she was stead-fastly determined to go with her, then she ceased speaking unto her.

"So they two went until they came to Bethlehem. And it came to pass, when they were come to Bethlehem, that all the city was moved about them,

31

and they said, Is this Naomi? And she said unto them, Call me not Naomi, call me Mara; for the Almighty hath dealt very bitterly with me. I went out full, and the Lord hath brought me home again empty. Why, then, call ye me Naomi, seeing the Lord hath testified against me, and the Almighty hath afflicted me? So Naomi returned, and Ruth, the Moabitess, her daughter-in-law, with her, who returned out of the country of Moab; and they came to Bethlehem in the beginning of barley harvest" (Ruth 1:15-22).

This is a key point in the story. If Ruth had not declared her faith, that would have been the end of the story. If Ruth had turned around and gone back to Moab and if Naomi had gone back to Bethlehem alone, the Book of Ruth would never have been written. We find a very important name at the end of the Book of Ruth—David. Through the family of David the Saviour came into the world. Little did Ruth and Naomi realize the importance of the decision Ruth made.

All of our decisions are important, but some have greater consequences than others. Ruth made one of the most important decisions of her life by declaring her faith. It is never easy to stand up and declare your faith, but if you ever hope to put your life together, you must do so.

A Believing Decision

In Ruth 1:15-22 we find three testimonies that encourage us to stand up and declare our faith in God. Let's begin with the testimony of Ruth. I like to call this testimony *a believing decision*. Only two good decisions are recorded in chapter 1 of the Book of Ruth: the decision Naomi made to return to Bethlehem and the decision Ruth made to go with her, thereby declaring her faith in God. Every other decision in this chapter was wrong.

In the midst of all these wrong decisions, Ruth, the Moabitess, made a right decision and declared her faith. What did Ruth reveal by this wonderful statement of her faith? First of all, she revealed her faithfulness to Naomi. We often hear jokes about mothers-in-law, but this daughter-in-law dearly loved her mother-in-law. In spite of Naomi's bad example, bad advice and bitter spirit, Ruth said, "I am going to stay with you" (see vv. 16,17). She declared her faithfulness to Naomi, a faithfulness unto death.

Those of us who know Jesus Christ as our Saviour ought to have this kind of commitment to one another. I think this is a beautiful statement of commitment for a husband and wife. Too many people today get married for better or for worse but not for long! They don't really make a commitment to one another. I think commitment is also important in our Christian ministry. Some believers will teach a Sunday school class until it becomes difficult—then they quit. Or they may join the choir until the rehearsal schedule gets hectic—then they quit. A pastor may take a church until problems appear—then he resigns.

Ruth is an example to us of commitment, of faithfulness unto death. Our Lord Jesus Christ is the greatest example of commitment. He was "obe-

33

dient unto death, even the death of the cross" (Phil. 2:8).

By her statement of faith, Ruth also declared that she had a brand-new family. "Where thou lodgest, I will lodge: thy people shall be my people" (Ruth 1:16). She was born and raised in Moab, but now she identified with God's people, the Jews. However, this decision presented a problem. Deuteronomy 23:3 says, "An Ammonite or Moabite shall not enter into the congregation of the Lord; even to their tenth generation shall they not enter into the congregation of the Lord forever." This was an obstacle that had to be overcome, but love and grace would overcome it. Ruth, by herself, could not enter the family of the people of Israel, but Boaz could do it for her. This is a beautiful picture of how love, grace and sacrifice brought this stranger into the family of God.

Ruth's statement of faith also declared her belief in the true God: "Thy God [shall be] my God" (Ruth 1:16). In Ruth 2:12 Boaz stated that Ruth had taken refuge under the wings of the God of Israel, whom she had come to trust. She turned her back on the idols of Moab and trusted the true God.

Ruth had a great deal of faith and determination. Ruth 1:18 says that she was steadfastly determined to go with Naomi. She was not going to quit! I admire that kind of commitment. She was not half-hearted, in spite of all the pressures against her. Ruth made a believing decision and declared her faith in God. That's the first testimony that should encourage us.

If a young woman raised in a heathen land, who worshiped idols, who had been through such heartache and sorrows, whose mother-in-law was such a bad example, could have this kind of faith, how much more faith should you and I have since we haven't had to overcome these obstacles!

A Bitter Disposition

Naomi's testimony was one of *a bitter disposition* because she blamed God. When she arrived in Bethlehem, the women said, "Is this Naomi?" (Ruth 1:19). They could tell by looking at her that she had been suffering. She told them, "Don't call me pleasant (Naomi); call me bitter (Mara)" (see v. 20). Why? Because "the Almighty hath dealt very bitterly with me" (v. 20). Naomi felt that God's hand had been against her (v. 13) and that He had afflicted her (v. 21) because she had gone out full but come home empty (v. 21). She had gone to Moab with a husband and two sons and had come home a childless widow.

Perhaps you are bitter at life and at God. You may be saying, "God has been cruel to me." Of course, this is impossible, for God cannot be cruel. Whatever He does is done in love, even though we may not see it that way. "But I don't understand what He's doing," you may argue. He didn't promise that we would always understand, but He is still in control and knows what is best for us. Bitterness is foolish. Your bitterness does not harm or change God, and it will not make the situation any better.

At the beginning of Ruth 1, Naomi made a wrong

35

decision. In the middle of the chapter, she gave wrong advice. By the end of the chapter, she had a wrong disposition. She became a backslidden woman who was bitter against God, but she was only hurting herself.

I have met people who have carried the poison of bitterness in their hearts for years. They were bitter against God because of something that had happened in their home or in their marriage or in their church. Bitterness only makes the situation worse and causes you to become miserable.

A Blessed Discipline

The third testimony we will examine is God's testimony of *a blessed discipline*. In Ruth 1:21 Naomi admitted, "The Lord hath testified against me." He testified against her unbelief and disobedience, against her running away and against her plan to cover up her sins. How did He do it? By converting Ruth. Ruth's conversion was a testimony against Naomi.

God, in His love, chastens us. Hebrews 12:6 says, "Whom the Lord loveth he chasteneth." When God chastens us, He is not simply punishing us for our disobedience. Chastening means "child training." God wants to build us up, help us to develop and train us. We can treat this discipline lightly and lose God's blessing as Orpah did. She didn't take the discipline seriously but left the family and went back home. Or we, like Naomi, can rebel against God's discipline. Instead of admitting her sin and seeing the purpose behind God's punishment, she blamed

God and believed that He was treating her unfairly. Little did Naomi realize that God was working *for* her and that through Ruth her life would be put back together again.

You can treat God's discipline lightly, you can rebel against it, or you can submit to it. Ruth submitted to the discipline of God. You don't find Ruth saying bitter things against God or feeling sorry for herself. She believed that God had a purpose in her suffering.

Naomi returned to Bethlehem a bitter and empty woman. Her bitterness showed on her face and in her words. She was not even thankful that Ruth had chosen to remain with her so she didn't have to be alone. But Ruth was grateful; she was thankful that she had found a new home and could make a new start. She was grateful that she could trust the living God. The Lord was preparing everything for them. It was the beginning of the barley harvest, and God had arranged for Ruth to glean in the fields of Boaz. Boaz would fall in love with Ruth, and everything would work out for God's glory and for their good.

God, in His providence, is working in your life today, whether you realize it or not. God has prepared blessings for you if you will only trust Him. What is your testimony today? Are you bitter? Are you angry at God? Are you blaming other people? Naomi was bitter, while Ruth believed in God and quietly trusted Him.

What is God's testimony about you today? Is God having to discipline you? Don't treat it lightly or rebel against it. If you want to put your life together,

37

get rid of bitterness, submit yourself to God and let Him work in your behalf. Declare your faith in the all-powerful God, and He will make you a living testimony to the world.

Chapter 5

A Change for the Better
(Ruth 2:1-7)

Naomi's life was torn apart because she and her family acted in unbelief. They tried to run away from their problems, but their problems only became worse. Then Naomi tried to cover up her disobedience, but her plan failed when Ruth declared her faith in God and chose to go to Bethlehem, despite Naomi's bad advice. When Naomi arrived in Bethlehem, she was a bitter woman because she blamed God for her trials. How did God put Naomi's life back together again? God often uses other believers as instruments to do His work in our lives. In this case He used Ruth, even though she was a young believer. Ruth's faith and love made the difference in Naomi's life.

As you move from the first to the second chapter of the Book of Ruth, the atmosphere changes dramatically. Notice the changes that take place because of Ruth's faith and love: "And Naomi had a kinsman of her husband's, a mighty man of wealth,

of the family of Elimelech; and his name was Boaz.
And Ruth, the Moabitess, said unto Naomi, Let me
now go to the field, and glean ears of grain after him
in whose sight I shall find grace. And she said unto
her, Go, my daughter. And she went, and came,
and gleaned in the field after the reapers; and she
happened to come to a portion of the field belonging
unto Boaz, who was of the kindred of Elimelech.

"And, behold, Boaz came from Bethlehem, and
said unto the reapers, The Lord be with you. And
they answered him, The Lord bless thee. Then said
Boaz unto his servant who was set over the reapers,
Whose damsel is this? And the servant who was set
over the reapers answered and said, It is the Moab-
itish damsel who came back with Naomi out of the
country of Moab. And she said, I pray you, let me
glean and gather after the reapers among the
sheaves. So she came, and hath continued even
from the morning until now, except that she tarried
a little in the house" (Ruth 2:1-7).

From Unbelief to Faith

The first change we see in Ruth 2:1-7 is a change
from unbelief to faith. Ruth was gaining an understanding of the Word of God and was claiming her
privilege to glean as stated in the Law: "When ye
reap the harvest of your land, thou shalt not wholly
reap the corners of thy field, neither shalt thou
gather the gleanings of thy harvest. And thou shalt
not glean thy vineyard, neither shalt thou gather
every grape of thy vineyard; thou shalt leave them

for the poor and sojourner: I am the Lord your God" (Lev. 19:9,10; see also 23:22; Deut. 24:19).

Naomi and Ruth knew about this regulation in the Word of God, and so Ruth claimed her privileges as a poor stranger in the land. She was living by faith, trusting God to care for her. She said to herself, *Since God has given this instruction in His Word, if I obey it by faith, then in grace He will lead me and provide for me.* She said to her mother-in-law, "Let me now go to the field and glean ears of grain after someone who will be kind to me" (Ruth 2:2, literal translation). She did not know where she was going or how she would be received. She simply believed the Word of God.

Why did she do this? She was thinking of Naomi, who was older and had experienced a great deal of difficulty. Ruth thought about others. One of the best ways to cure discouragement and despondency is to do something for someone else. John Keble, a British preacher of a century ago, wrote: "When you find yourself overpowered as it were by melancholy, the best way is to go out and do something kind to somebody or other." I think this is good advice. Naomi was bitter and feeling sorry for herself; but Ruth went out into the fields to glean, trusting in the Word of God. Faith always leads to works. "Faith without works is dead" (James 2:20).

In Ruth 1 we see an atmosphere of unbelief. When the famine came to Bethlehem, Elimelech and his family left for Moab in unbelief. Naomi's two sons married women of Moab, an act of unbelief. Naomi tried to cover up her disobedience in unbe-

41

lief. But in chapter 2 we see Ruth living by faith. If you want to put your life together, you must start living and acting by faith. Find out what the Word of God says, and obey it. When you do, God will begin to work.

From Rebellion to Submission

Not only do we see a change from unbelief to faith, but we also note a change *from rebellion to submission*. Naomi had been rebellious. She and her husband had rebelled against God by going to Moab. She had rebelled when she allowed her sons to marry Moabites, when she sent Orpah back home and when she tried to force Ruth to return. No wonder Naomi had such a bitter spirit! Rebellion always leads to bitterness.

Notice how Ruth, by contrast, practiced submission, even though Naomi was rebellious and bitter. We see in Ruth 2:2 that she didn't act as an independent agent. She didn't walk out of the house saying, "Well, I think I'll go out and find something to do!" No, she went to her mother-in-law (who was in charge of the home), submitted herself to Naomi and asked permission to go to the field. Rebellion always destroys and tears things apart, but submission has a way of putting things back together again.

Ruth also submitted to the reapers. When she came to the field, she very graciously and humbly went to the reapers and said, "I pray you, let me glean and gather after the reapers among the sheaves" (v. 7). The man in charge of the field gave her permission to do so. She had the Word of God to defend her, but she still acted in a sweet and gracious manner.

This reminds me of Daniel. When he refused to eat the king's food because it was dedicated to idols and was not part of his diet as a Jew, he did not make a big fuss about it (see Dan. 1:8-16). He went to the man in charge and talked to him graciously. They made an arrangement to test the simple food that Daniel and his friends requested.

Christians do not need to become haughty and demanding just because they have the Word of God to back them up. We should always be "swift to hear, slow to speak, slow to wrath" (James 1:19).

Ruth submitted to Naomi, to the man in charge of the reapers and then to Boaz. When she met Boaz, he called her "my daughter" (Ruth 2:8). He was very kind to her. "Then she fell on her face, and bowed herself to the ground, and said unto him, Why have I found grace in thine eyes, that thou shouldest take knowledge of me, seeing I am a foreigner?" (v. 10). She did not know who he was or what he could do for her—she found that out later from Naomi—but she knew that he was in charge, and so she submitted to him.

Because Ruth was submissive to the Lord and to others, God began to work in her behalf. He led Ruth and made sure that she and Naomi had enough to eat. She "happened" to come to a portion of the field belonging to Boaz. This was not an accident—it was an appointment. When you submit to the Lord and to others, God will lead you and feed you.

From Bitterness to Gratitude

The third change we see in Ruth 2 is a difference in attitude. The attitude has changed *from bitterness to gratitude*. Ruth could easily have given in to feelings of bitterness and anger. After all, she had lost her father-in-law, her husband and her brother-in-law; then she lost her sister-in-law who went back home. She was poor, she was a widow, and she was a foreigner. She had a right to be bitter. It would have been easy for her to sit down with Naomi and say, "I'm going to sit here with you and complain!" But she didn't allow herself to become bitter because, unlike Naomi, she had faith in God and was willing to submit to Him. She could put the past behind her and faithfully trust God to take care of the future.

Naomi, on the other hand, was thinking only of herself and was living in the past. She chose to dwell on her sorrow and pain and feel sorry for herself instead of trusting God. She was out of fellowship with God and therefore was bitter, rebellious, ungrateful and very miserable.

Ruth was enjoying sweet fellowship with God because she was a woman who lived by *grace*. She realized that whatever she had was the gracious gift of God. She was grateful for what she received. In humility and gratitude she asked Boaz, "Why have I found grace in thine eyes, that thou shouldest take knowledge of me, seeing I am a foreigner?" (v. 10).

A truly satisfied person is one who goes through life thinking of others and who realizes that everything he has comes from the hand of God. John the Baptist said, "A man can receive nothing, except it be given him from heaven" (John 3:27). All of life is a gift from God.

From Emptiness to Satisfaction

The atmosphere of hopelessness and despair that prevailed in chapter 1 has been transformed into new hope, because God has begun to use Ruth as His instrument of change. The focus has shifted from Naomi, with her attitude of unbelief, rebellion and bitterness, to Ruth and her attitude of faith, submission and gratitude. The last change that takes place is a transformation *from emptiness to satisfaction.*

When Naomi came back to Bethlehem, she said, "I went out full, and the Lord hath brought me home again empty" (Ruth 1:21). She had an empty home—she had lost her husband and two sons. She had empty hands—she was poor and needy. She had an empty heart because she was bitter against God.

While Naomi is a picture of an empty life, Ruth is a picture of a person who is satisfied. She was satisfied with what God brought to her life and with the food that He placed before her. Ruth began by gathering the leftovers of the harvest and was grateful for the small portion she had. God rewarded her for her faithfulness and thankfulness. He led her to Boaz who allowed her to eat from his own table until she was completely satisfied (see 2:14). Then Boaz

45

instructed the reapers to purposely drop extra grain for her in the field (see v. 16). Ruth's hands were not empty—God met her every need. Her heart was not empty, for it was filled with gratitude, love and faith. She loved God and Naomi. God will bless that love when Boaz falls in love with her. From this point on, the emphasis is not on Ruth's love for Naomi but on Ruth and Boaz and their love for each other.

Naomi is a good example of a spiritually bankrupt person. The formula for her life was *unbelief* plus *rebellion* plus *bitterness* equals *emptiness*. Ruth, on the other hand, is a model of a person who is spiritually rich. She discovered the many blessings to be found in living by the rule: *faith* plus *submission* plus *gratitude* equals *satisfaction*. God, in His providence, led her, fed her and changed her life for the better. She had no idea of the wonderful plan that He had for her life.

Not only does Ruth's life change for the better, but through Ruth, Naomi's life is affected as well. Naomi's bitterness will be replaced with blessedness as her empty home, hands and heart are once again filled with a family, food and faith. Instead of hopelessness, these women have a living hope, as God begins to put their lives back together again.

If your life is falling apart, it is likely that you are part of the problem. We have seen that unbelief, rebellion and bitterness only lead to emptiness. You can continue to tear things apart by your bad attitude, or you can change your life for the better by submitting to God and allowing Him to work through you. May the Lord help all of us to be like Ruth, a woman of faith, submission and gratitude— a satisfied person who is putting things together for the glory of God.

Chapter 6

Here Comes the Bridegroom!
(Ruth 2:8-16)

When Naomi and Ruth arrived in Bethlehem, the barley harvest was beginning. It would have been early spring, probably April. It would have been a time of rejoicing over the fruitfulness of the harvest. When Ruth went out to glean in the field, God providentially led her to the field of Boaz. Little did she realize that one day she would be the wife of this mighty man. We never know where even the "little decisions" of life will lead us if we are in the will of God.

"Then said Boaz unto Ruth, Hearest thou not, my daughter? Go not to glean in another field, neither go from here, but abide here close by my maidens; let thine eyes be on the field that they do reap, and go thou after them. Have I not charged the young men that they shall not touch thee? And when thou art thirsty, go unto the vessels, and drink of that which the young men have drawn. Then she fell on her face, and bowed herself to the ground, and said unto him, Why have I found grace in thine eyes, that thou shouldest take knowledge of me, seeing I am a foreigner?

"And Boaz answered and said unto her, It hath

fully been shown me, all that thou hast done for thy mother-in-law since the death of thine husband, and how thou hast left thy father and thy mother, and the land of thy nativity, and art come unto a people whom thou knewest not heretofore. The Lord recompense thy work, and a full reward be given thee by the Lord God of Israel, under whose wings thou art come to trust. Then she said, Let me find favor in thy sight, my lord; for thou hast comforted me, and because thou hast spoken friendly unto thine handmaid, though I be not like unto one of thine handmaidens. And Boaz said unto her, At mealtime come thou here, and eat of the bread, and dip thy morsel in the vinegar. And she sat beside the reapers; and he reached her parched grain, and she did eat, and was satisfied, and left. And when she got up to glean, Boaz commanded his young men, saying, Let her glean even among the sheaves, and reproach her not; and let fall also some of the handfuls on purpose for her, and leave them, that she may glean them, and rebuke her not" (Ruth 2:8-16).

Boaz, of course, is a beautiful picture of our Lord Jesus Christ. The name Boaz means "mighty man," and Christ is "The Mighty God" (Isa. 9:6). As soon as Boaz appeared on the scene, Ruth became the object of his attention and affection. I have a feeling that Boaz took one look at her and fell in love. Now that Boaz was watching over Ruth, she had nothing to fear.

Ruth enjoyed many blessings because of what Boaz did. We can enjoy those same blessings if we have trusted Jesus Christ as our Saviour.

The Blessing of Guidance

First of all, Ruth experienced *the blessing of guidance*. Boaz said, "Go not to glean in another field, neither go from here, but abide here close by my maidens" (Ruth 2:8). Ruth needed guidance, for there were no markers, mailboxes, names or addresses in the fields of Bethlehem! The people of Israel knew where the boundaries were, but Ruth was a stranger. In fact, she found her way to the field of Boaz because of the providential leading of God.

Boaz told her to stay in his field. Ruth was an inexperienced gleaner, a young widow with no one to guide her. Someone could jokingly give her wrong counsel and lead her astray, so Boaz watched over her.

I feel sorry for those who do not know Jesus Christ as their Saviour. How do they receive guidance? The Word of God promises in Psalm 32:8, "I [God] will guide thee with mine eye." Proverbs 3:5,6 says, "Trust in the Lord with all thine heart, and lean not unto thine own understanding. In all thy ways acknowledge him, and he shall direct thy paths." God guides those who belong to Him and who will submit to Him.

In Ruth 1 Elimelech and his family did not seek the guidance of God, and they reaped the consequences. Ruth, because she was following the guidance of Boaz, avoided trouble.

The Blessing of Protection

Ruth also enjoyed *the blessing of protection*. Boaz told her, "Let thine eyes be on the field that they do reap, and go thou after them. Have I not charged the young men that they shall not touch thee?" (Ruth 2:9). Ruth was young, and we get the impression that she was attractive. She was also a widow and a foreigner. Some people would not respect her because she was a Moabitess. Also, because it was harvest season, much celebrating and revelry and even some misbehaving would occur. Ruth could have been in danger, but Boaz was now protecting her.

Boaz told Ruth, "Stay close to my maidens" (v. 8). He had told his maidens to watch over her, and he had also warned the young men not to touch her. Some of them might be tempted, but they knew that Boaz would act swiftly and surely. So Ruth was protected by the fellowship of the young women and by the warning given to the young men.

Christians need the protection of fellowship. I meet people who claim they can survive without the local church. I don't think they can. We need the fellowship of God's people—believers who will walk with us, guide us and rebuke us if necessary.

God is watching over us. When a believer is in the will of God, he has the Lord's protection and guidance. God will give His angels charge over us to keep us in all His ways (see Ps. 91:11). "God is our refuge and strength, a very present help in trouble" (Ps. 46:1). We can rest in the assurance that God will be there to protect and strengthen us in troubled times. Even though we may not understand the reasons behind our suffering, we have the promise that "all things work together for good to

51

them that love God, to them who are the called according to his purpose" (Rom. 8:28).

The Blessing of Provision

Ruth was blessed with the guidance and protection of Boaz. She also received *the blessing of provision.* Boaz not only allowed her to glean in his field, but he also told the young men, "If she wants to glean among the sheaves, don't reproach her. And deliberately drop some grain for her to pick up" (see Ruth 2:15,16). The Mosaic Law only required that they not go back over their fields and pick up what was dropped. The Law also said they should not reap in the corners of the field but leave it for the poor. Boaz went beyond the Law. He told the reapers to drop some handfuls on purpose for Ruth to gather.

Boaz provided grain for Ruth to glean. He also provided water for her to drink: "When thou art thirsty, go unto the vessels, and drink of that which the young men have drawn" (v. 9). He even allowed her to eat at his table: "At mealtime come thou here, and eat of the bread, and dip thy morsel in the vinegar" (v. 14).

Our Lord provides for our needs. "God shall supply all your need according to his riches in glory by Christ Jesus" (Phil. 4:19). In Matthew 6 the Lord rebukes us for worrying. He said, in effect, "Your Heavenly Father takes care of the lilies of the field and makes them beautiful, so why are you worrying about clothing yourself? If He feeds the birds and protects them, why are you worrying about what you are going to eat and drink? Your Father knows what you need even before you ask" (see vv. 25-32). Christ promised that when we seek God's kingdom and righteousness first, all that we need will be supplied (see v. 33). God provides for our every need, as we obey Him.

The Blessing of Encouragement

The fourth blessing that Ruth experienced because of Boaz was *the blessing of encouragement*. Ruth said to Boaz, "Let me find favor in thy sight, my lord; for thou hast comforted me, and because thou hast spoken friendly unto thine handmaid" (Ruth 2:13). The Hebrew text reads: "Thou hast spoken to the heart of thine handmaiden." Boaz didn't simply speak to her ears; he spoke to her heart. He said to her, "You don't have to be afraid. You shouldn't worry. I am in control, and I will take care of all your needs." He comforted and encouraged her by the words he spoke.

Where do you turn for encouragement? Some people, when they are experiencing difficulty, try to find encouragement in a bottle, in a pill or needle, or in some worldly pleasure. These things may provide a temporary escape from problems, but they do not serve to encourage or help the person. They only make him more depressed. The Christian can find true encouragement in the promises of the Bible. "For whatever things were written in earlier times were written for our learning, that we, through patience and comfort of the scriptures, might have hope" (Rom. 15:4). Ruth found her encouragement in the words of Boaz, and we find our encouragement in God's Word.

The Blessing of Fellowship

In the house of Boaz, Ruth found guidance, protection, provision and encouragement. She also found *the blessing of fellowship*. Boaz extended to Ruth the most gracious invitation in the Bible—the invitation to come and dine with him and his servants. "Come thou here, and eat of the bread, and dip thy morsel in the vinegar. And she sat beside the reapers; and he [Boaz] reached her parched grain, and she did eat, and was satisfied" (Ruth 2:14). We have already seen that Boaz provided for Ruth's physical needs by feeding her, but allowing her to eat at his table also gave her some much needed fellowship. Boaz made Ruth feel welcome, loved and spiritually nourished.

Boaz knew that Ruth needed the fellowship of others to strengthen her new-found faith in God. Christians also need the fellowship of other believers and of Christ Himself in order to grow. Just as Boaz nourished Ruth, so also the Lord Jesus nourishes us. He gives us food for our souls that satisfies us. Are you in fellowship today with the Lord Jesus Christ? Have you accepted His invitation to come and dine, to sit with Him at His table?

The Blessing of Acceptance

Ruth received a sixth blessing through Boaz—*the blessing of acceptance*. Boaz spoke to the young men and said, "Reproach her not" (Ruth 2:15). He also told them, "Rebuke her not" (v. 16). In other words, they were not to treat her like a foreigner, a widow or a poor woman; they were to accept her. Everything was *against* Ruth's being accepted. To begin with, she was a foreigner, a Moabitess. That meant she could not be received into the congregation of God even to the tenth generation (see Deut. 23:3). She was an outsider—outside the promises and the covenants given to God's people. She was also a *woman* in a society pretty much dominated by the *men*. And she was a widow, which meant she was helpless. Next to orphans, I don't know of anyone in Israel who would be in a more helpless position than a poor widow. Some of the smart young men who were reaping in the field might have been tempted to taunt this poor foreigner, but they didn't dare. Boaz said, "I have accepted her, so you treat her the way I would treat her. Don't insult her, reproach her or rebuke her."

We can rejoice that in spite of our background— where we came from, what we might have done or who we are—we have been accepted by Jesus Christ, "accepted in the Beloved"! (Eph. 1:6).

The Blessing of Satisfaction

The seventh blessing was *the blessing of satisfaction.* "She [Ruth] did eat, and was satisfied" (Ruth 2:14). Her *past* was forgotten; she had now been accepted and was not being treated like a stranger. Her *future* was full of hope because someone cared for her. Her *present* needs were being met, so she was satisfied. I doubt that she had ever been satis-

55

fied in Moab because Moab is a picture of the world, and the world does not offer any satisfaction. People of the world claim they are satisfied, but really they are not.

The only true satisfaction comes from the Lord Jesus Christ. He said to the woman at the well, "If you drink of this water, you will be thirsty again; but if you drink of the water that I can give you, you will never thirst again" (John 4:13,14).

Did you notice that all of Ruth's blessings were the result of *grace* and *faith?* Ruth told Naomi she would glean in the person's field "in whose sight I shall find grace" (Ruth 2:2). Ruth later asked Boaz, "Why have I found grace in thine eyes?" (v. 10). After Boaz expressed his acceptance of Ruth, she remarked, "Let me find favor in thy sight" (v. 13). Ruth was living by grace. Ruth also lived by faith. Boaz said of her, "The Lord recompense thy work, and a full reward be given thee by the Lord God of Israel, under whose wings thou art come to trust" (v. 12). Ruth was living "by grace through faith." She had entered into fellowship with God, and she was now truly satisfied.

When we live by grace through faith, we can enjoy the same blessings that Ruth enjoyed. Just as Boaz met all the needs Ruth had, the Lord Jesus Christ will meet all of our needs. We can experience His guidance, protection, provision, encouragement, fellowship, acceptance and satisfaction. What riches we have in Christ!

Chapter 7

From Bitterness to Blessing
(Ruth 2:17-23)

What a difference one day can make in your life! One April day in 1945, the late president Harry S. Truman wrote to his mother: "I had hurried to the White House to see the president, and when I got there, I found out I *was* the president."

Moses once began his day as a shepherd and ended it as a prophet, a prophet of God who had heard His voice (see Ex. 3,4). David went out one day to take food to his brothers in Saul's army; and before the day ended, he was a hero because he had slain Goliath (see I Sam. 17:17-58). Peter allowed Jesus to use his boat one day; and before the day was over, he abandoned everything to follow the Lord Jesus Christ and become His disciple (see Luke 5:1-11). What a difference one day can make!

Today can make a difference in your life. How today will affect the rest of your life depends on what you do with your day, what decisions you make.

One day made a great difference in Ruth's life too. She went into the fields one day to glean and found herself the object of the attention and affection of a man named Boaz. At that time, Ruth did not know who Boaz was, but she certainly found out when she arrived home and gave the news to Naomi.

"So she gleaned in the field until evening, and beat out what she had gleaned; and it was about an ephah of barley. And she took it up, and went into the city. And her mother-in-law saw what she had gleaned; and she brought out and gave to her what she had reserved after she was satisfied. And her mother-in-law said unto her, Where hast thou gleaned today? And where wroughtest thou? [Where did you work?] Blessed be he that did take knowledge of thee. And she showed her mother-in-law with whom she had wrought, and said, The man's name with whom I wrought today is Boaz.

"And Naomi said unto her daughter-in-law, Blessed be he of the Lord, who hath not withheld his kindness to the living and to the dead. And Naomi said unto her, The man is near of kin unto us, one of our next kinsmen. And Ruth, the Moabitess, said, He said unto me also, Thou shalt keep close by my young men, until they have ended all my harvest. And Naomi said unto Ruth, her daughter-in-law, It is good, my daughter, that thou go out with his maidens, that they meet thee not in any other field. So she kept close by the maidens of Boaz to glean until the end of barley harvest and of wheat harvest, and dwelt with her mother-in-law" (Ruth 2:17-23).

Did you notice that Naomi is now starting to change? She is no longer the bitter widow we met in chapter 1. Her life was falling apart, but now God is putting her life back together again. What made the difference? Boaz has arrived on the scene.

A New Word on Naomi's Lips

Three new factors enter the story because of the arrival of Boaz. First of all, *a new word is on Naomi's lips,* the word "blessed." She hasn't used that word before, but now she does. "Blessed be he that did take knowledge of thee" (Ruth 2:19). "Blessed be he of the Lord, who hath not withheld his kindness to the living and to the dead" (v. 20).

Previously, Naomi has been bitter—bitter because of her empty home, her empty heart and her empty hands. She found nothing to rejoice in. But now she is using this new word "blessed." Why? Because she saw the food Ruth had brought from her day's labor. Ruth had gleaned almost a bushel of barley, and she had also brought Naomi some of the parched grain and table food that was left over after she had eaten with Boaz.

When Naomi saw the food, she said, "Blessed be he of the Lord" (v. 20). She graciously admitted that Boaz had been kind and that the Lord had been at work. The name of the Lord is once again on Naomi's lips, but this time she blesses the Lord with her words instead of speaking about Him bitterly and blaming Him for her problems.

Naomi's life is beginning to change. She had been worried about the emptiness of her life and how she would survive, but now she can see the food that God has provided. Before, her life had looked hopeless. What future did two widows have in Bethle-

59

hem? But now Boaz has come on the scene and is showing an interest in Ruth.

Are you feeling very discouraged or even bitter toward God? Are you looking at your past and saying, "I've wrecked everything. My whole life is being torn apart and is falling to pieces"? The present may seem unbearable to you, and your future may look even worse; but remember one thing—when Jesus Christ steps into the picture, everything changes. Jesus Christ, our Boaz, is here to help us just as He helped Ruth. The Lord, through Boaz, protected Ruth, provided for her needs and promised to take care of her. As a result, Ruth's and Naomi's lives started to change. Naomi's bitterness turned into blessedness, her emptiness became fullness, and her discouragement turned into hope. Naomi now has a new word on her lips. It's the word "blessed."

I don't think that you and I use the word "blessed" enough. We pray for the Lord's blessings for ourselves, but rarely do we bless the Lord with our lips and heart. We need to be like the psalmist, who said, "Bless the Lord, O my soul, and all that is within me, bless his holy name. Bless the Lord, O my soul, and forget not all his benefits" (Ps. 103:1,2).

A New Hope in Naomi's Heart

Not only is there a new word on Naomi's lips, but there is also *a new hope in Naomi's heart.* Naomi and Ruth had three reasons to be encouraged and hopeful. The first reason we see in this passage is their realization of *who Boaz was*—their kinsman.

Thirteen times in the Book of Ruth you find references to the "kinsman." The law of the kinsman-redeemer is found in Leviticus 25:25. This law stated that if a Jew became poor and had to sell his property or had to sell himself into slavery, one of his kinsmen could redeem him. The kinsman could pay the price and redeem the person and his property. A second law that applied to the kinsman-redeemer is found in Deuteronomy 25:5-10. It had to do with marriage. The law said that if a man died, his brother was required to marry the widow and raise the firstborn child in the name of the dead man. The kinsman was also required to maintain the man's inheritance until the child was old enough to receive it.

Naomi saw these two laws combined in Boaz, their kinsman. He could marry Ruth and raise children according to the law of Deuteronomy 25, and he could also redeem Ruth and her property, thus obeying the law in Leviticus 25. Naomi and Ruth had a new hope because of who Boaz was. They now had the promise of a redeemer.

The second reason Naomi had a new hope is because of *what Boaz did*. What did he do? He took a personal interest in Ruth. Out of all the people who were working in his field, he noticed Ruth and spoke to her. But more than that, he protected her and provided for her generously. He told the reapers to purposely drop some handfuls of grain for her to glean. When Naomi saw all the grain that Ruth had gathered, she was amazed. She knew that someone had been extra kind to Ruth. Then she found out that it was Boaz who had helped Ruth, and she realized that he could do much more for them.

Naomi was encouraged by who Boaz was and by what he did. She had a third reason for hope because of *what Boaz said*. Ruth remembered the words that he had spoken to her: "Thou shalt keep close by my young men, until they have ended all my harvest" (Ruth 2:21). I believe he was saying to her, "At the end of the harvest, something special is going to happen. Stay in my field until the harvest is over. My men will protect you." Boaz had some special plans in mind once he completed the harvest. Ruth remembered his words, and she and Naomi were encouraged by them.

Naomi was given new hope because of what Boaz had done, what he had said and what he could do for them as their kinsman-redeemer. We have this same hope because of what Jesus, our Kinsman-Redeemer, has done and will do for us. His salvation and promises for our life are real.

A New Motive in Ruth's Service

The third new factor that has entered the story is *a new motive in Ruth's service*. Ruth could have stayed at home and waited for Boaz to perform his duties as kinsman-redeemer, but she didn't do this. Instead, she went right back to the field and labored. She gleaned during the barley harvest and then worked on through the wheat harvest. This meant that she would have worked from April until about June. But I believe that Ruth went back to the

62

field with a new attitude and purpose because the situation was different. Now, she knew the lord of the harvest!

Notice in Ruth 2:21 that Boaz called it "my harvest." He was the lord of the harvest. Ruth was now more that just a laborer in the field; she was loved by the lord of the harvest! He spoke to her and invited her to his table to eat. He cared for her and had plans for her. Ruth's labor was not the dismal labor of a slave—it was the buoyant, joyful labor of someone who had great expectations.

You and I should follow Ruth's example as we serve in the field. Ruth is a beautiful picture of the ideal servant. She said, "Let me now go to the field" (v. 2). She willingly volunteered to serve Naomi by gleaning, even though it was a hard and often unrewarding task. Is God calling you to find a place of ministry? Are you willingly serving Him in the field? Jesus said, "Lift up your eyes, and look on the fields; for they are white already to harvest" (John 4:35). It is so easy to become distracted. Perhaps you are discouraged because the work is not going the way you would like it to. But God says to you, as Boaz said to Ruth, "Let thine eyes be on the field" (Ruth 2:9). Keep your eyes on the field and keep working in the Lord's harvest, because God has placed you there for a reason.

Notice in verse 17 that Ruth gleaned in the field until evening. She made good use of the time she had to work. Our Lord said, "The night cometh, when no man can work" (John 9:4). Our opportunities will be gone someday. You and I cannot depend

63

on any time except today to do the work of God. We must do all we can while there is still time.

Ruth had a hope for the harvest. The harvest belonged to Boaz, and she was sharing in his wealth as well as in his work. You and I don't have to be afraid or ashamed. We are laboring in the field, and we know a harvest is coming. "Let us not be weary in well doing; for in due season we shall reap, if we faint not" (Gal. 6:9).

If you are bitter and your life seems to be falling apart, fix your eyes on Jesus Christ, the Lord of the Harvest. He is your Boaz, your mighty man of wealth. Consider all that He is to you and all that He has done for you. If you and I will just keep our eyes on the Lord Jesus, if we will do our work the way He wants us to do it, before long we will be saying with David, "Bless the Lord, O my soul, and all that is within me, bless his holy name" (Ps. 103:1).

Chapter 8

The Turning Points of Life
(Ruth 3:1-7)

In Ruth 3 we see that Naomi has become a different person. She has put away her bitterness and selfishness and is more concerned about Ruth than about herself. Naomi's supreme desire now is that Ruth might have a happy future, which means finding her a husband.

"Then Naomi, her mother-in-law, said unto her, My daughter, shall I not seek rest for thee, that it may be well with thee? And now is not Boaz of our kindred, with whose maidens thou wast? Behold, he winnoweth barley tonight in the threshing floor. Wash thyself, therefore, and anoint thyself, and put thy raiment upon thee, and get thee down to the floor; but make not thyself known unto the man, until he shall have finished eating and drinking. And it shall be, when he lieth down, that thou shalt mark the place where he shall lie, and thou shalt go in, and uncover his feet, and lie down; and he will tell thee what thou shalt do. And she said unto her, All that thou sayest unto me I will do.

"And she went down unto the floor, and did according to all that her mother-in-law bade her.

And when Boaz had eaten and drunk, and his heart was merry, he went to lie down at the end of the heap of grain; and she came softly, and uncovered his feet, and lay down" (Ruth 3:1-7).

The word "rest" in verse 1 means "to be settled in life." Ruth was young and needed a husband; but she came from Moab, and the Moabites were not accepted in the nation of Israel. Boaz was Ruth and Naomi's only hope for solving their problems and putting their lives together again. Naomi told Ruth the plan; but in order for this plan to work, Ruth had to fulfill some definite conditions. If you want to put your life together, you must fulfill these same conditions in a spiritual way.

We Must Have the Right Purpose

First of all, *we must have the right purpose.* Ruth's purpose for going to the threshing floor and lying at the feet of Boaz was to establish a *lasting* relationship with him. In Ruth 1, Ruth did not even know that Boaz existed. In chapter 2 she saw him only as her benefactor, the one who fed her and protected her. Then she discovered that Boaz was really a relative, a near kinsman who could redeem her. Now Ruth wanted to establish a permanent relationship with him. She wanted him to be more than a benefactor, who would give her gifts; she desired a bridegroom, who would share his life and his love with her.

Too many Christians want to put their lives together just to escape problems or to receive blessings and benefits. Naomi and Ruth had the right purpose in mind. Ruth wanted to give herself and her love completely to Boaz. We must have this same purpose for our lives—to totally commit ourselves to the Lord Jesus Christ. Our relationship with the Lord must be more than just a casual friendship for the sole purpose of receiving His protection, blessings and provision. We must desire a deep, intimate relationship with Him. After all, the reason our lives fell apart to begin with was because we lacked a close relationship with Jesus Christ and disobeyed Him as a result.

Naomi realized that Ruth could not continue living the way she was. She was living on the leftovers of others (see v. 7), which would only provide barely enough to survive. But then Boaz began to give her handfuls of grain on purpose (see v. 16). He invited her to eat with his servants at his table and also gave her bountiful gifts that she brought home (see v. 14). But all of this was futile without a loving, living relationship with Boaz. By entering into a deeper relationship with Boaz, Ruth enjoyed not only the gifts but the giver! If all you want in life are the gifts that God has for you, then you never will really put your life together. But if you establish a deep, personal relationship with the Giver of every good and perfect gift (see James 1:17), then your life can really change.

We Must Go to the Right Person

The second condition we must fulfill if we want to put our life together is that *we must go to the right person.* Ruth could have fallen in love with and married another man if she had desired. She was young and attractive. She was a believer in the true God and had identified herself with the people of Israel. In fact, several young men had been watching her and were showing an interest in her (see Ruth 3:10). But Boaz was the kinsman-redeemer and, according to the Law, he had a right to redeem her and marry her. The Law required that the redeemer be a close relative who had the finances needed to redeem the person and property. Boaz was a wealthy man and had given every evidence that he loved Ruth and wanted to redeem her.

Jesus Christ is our Kinsman-Redeemer, and He alone is *able* to redeem us. He became our kinsman when He came to earth and took on Himself a human body so that He could become one with us. He "made himself of no reputation, and took upon him the form of a servant" (Phil. 2:7). What a price He paid to do that! He is also able to redeem us—in fact, He is the only One in the universe who could redeem us—because He is sinless. He is "holy, harmless, undefiled" (Heb. 7:26). He "knew no sin" (II Cor. 5:21); He "did no sin" (I Pet. 2:22). The Lord Jesus Christ is also able to redeem us because He was able to pay the price. What was the price of redemption? Hebrews 9:22 says, "Without shedding of blood is no remission [forgiveness of sins]." Christ shed His own precious blood for us.

But is Christ *willing* to redeem us? Certainly He is! Christ Himself said that no one could take His life from Him but that He would freely give it (see John 10:17,18). He is also willing to redeem anyone who will come. "For God so loved the world, that he gave his only begotten Son, that whosoever believeth in him should not perish, but have everlasting life" (John 3:16). He is the only One who can redeem us. "There is no other name under heaven given among men, whereby we must be saved" (Acts 4:12).

So Jesus Christ is the right Person—and the only Person—to dedicate your life to. What is your relationship to Him? Do you know Him as your Saviour and Lord? Have you totally committed your life to Him?

We Must Make the Right Preparations

A third condition we must meet to put our life together is that *we must make the right preparations.* Naomi told Ruth exactly how to prepare for her meeting with Boaz. Ruth's actions were not improper. Some people read all kinds of immorality into this event, but this is wrong. What Ruth did was the custom of that day. You may ask, "Why didn't Boaz propose to her?" To begin with, Boaz was older and didn't know whether or not Ruth would want an older man. He wasn't sure she cared for him. Also, another kinsman had first claim to the property and to Ruth (Ruth 3:12,13). Ruth had to act by faith. What she did was perfectly proper.

Naomi's instructions to Ruth have a spiritual application to us today. "Wash thyself, therefore, and anoint thyself, and put thy raiment upon thee, and get thee down to the floor" (v. 3). We are to present ourselves clean, attractive and acceptable to the Lord. As His people, we are to "change clothes" spiritually. In Colossians 3, Paul told us to take off the "grave clothes" of the old life and to put on the "grace clothes" of the new life. He exhorted us to put off such things as anger, blasphemy, lying and other sins that grieve the Holy Spirit (see vv. 8,9). He urged us to put on the beautiful garments of God's grace, such as tenderness, forgiveness and the rest of the fruit of the Spirit (see vv. 12-17).

In other words, Naomi was telling Ruth, "Take off your widow's garments. You have been wearing them long enough. Put on fresh clothes. We are no longer going to live in the past. We are going to live for the future."

"Wash thyself" (Ruth 3:3) suggests personal cleansing and holiness. "Having, therefore, these promises, dearly beloved, let us cleanse ourselves from all filthiness of the flesh and spirit, perfecting holiness in the fear of God" (II Cor. 7:1). It is one thing to ask God to wash us, but it is something else for us to *wash ourselves*. We must stop sinning and remove everything from our life that grieves the Lord. We must anoint ourselves with the fragrance of the Holy Spirit and present ourselves at the feet of Jesus.

Establishing a deeper relationship with a person always requires paying a price, doesn't it? Ruth could not come to Boaz any way she pleased. She had to prepare herself for this important meeting. God will not put your life together until you put off the old life and put on the new life. You must wash yourself and cleanse your heart and mind. Remove everything from your life that doesn't belong there, and place yourself at the feet of your Boaz, the Lord Jesus Christ.

We Must Be at the Right Place

The fourth condition we need to fulfill is that *we must be at the right place*. Four times in Ruth 3 the phrase "his feet" is used (vv. 4,7,8,14). Ruth was to go to the feet of her kinsman-redeemer, which was the place of total submission. She had been at his feet when she met him in the field: "Then she fell on her face, and bowed herself to the ground, and said unto him, Why have I found grace in thine eyes, that thou shouldest take knowledge of me, seeing I am a foreigner?" (2:10). She had knelt to thank him for his gifts, but now she would come to present herself to him.

This is the type of commitment referred to in Romans 12:1: "I beseech you therefore, brethren, by the mercies of God, that ye present your bodies a living sacrifice, holy, acceptable unto God, which is your reasonable service."

In Ruth 2, Boaz came to Ruth, but in chapter 3 Ruth went to Boaz. In chapter 2 Ruth fell at his feet because he was so kind to her, but in chapter 3 she came to him because she wanted *him* rather than his gifts. She wanted to blend her life with his life so that all he was and all that he had would become hers.

This act of dedication was done privately, not publicly. In fact, all of the plans were made privately, but the *purchasing* was done publicly. Boaz purchased Ruth and the property at the city gate with ten elders of the city as witnesses. This is also true of our salvation. All of the plans for our redemption were made privately in the counsels of eternity by God the Father, God the Son and God the Holy Spirit. But the price was paid publicly when the Lord Jesus died on the cross outside the city of Jerusalem.

By faith, Ruth had to come to the right place and submit herself to the right person, her kinsman-redeemer. She did not know what the future held, but she obeyed Naomi's instructions by faith: "Uncover his feet, and lie down; and he will tell thee what thou shalt do" (v. 4). It was probably chilly outside so that when Ruth uncovered his feet, Boaz would notice it. But when it came to doing what needed to be done, Boaz didn't have "cold feet" at all! He swiftly took care of the matter.

Ruth came for the right purpose, to the right person, having made the right preparations and putting herself in the right place. When we find Ruth at the feet of the lord of the harvest, this is the turning point in the whole story. From this point on, *Boaz* is busy. Ruth now rests and waits to see what Boaz will do. She trusts his word.

Have you come to the feet of the Lord of the Harvest? Have you responded to His invitation: "Come unto me, all ye that labor and are heavy laden, and I will give you rest"? (Matt. 11:28). Naomi told Ruth, "My daughter, shall I not seek rest for thee, that it may be well with thee?" (Ruth 3:1). We will find no rest until we come to Jesus Christ and submit to His lordship. This place of submission is the only place where God can begin to put our lives back together again. Let's not rebel or argue with God or worry about the future any longer. Let's cleanse our lives and present ourselves to Christ in humble submission.

Chapter 9

When Everything Becomes New!
(Ruth 3:8-18)

Life is sometimes filled with "rude awakenings." Some of these awakenings are pleasant, and some are unpleasant. Adam woke up and discovered that God had created a wife for him. Jacob woke up and discovered that he was married to the *wrong* wife! Boaz awoke at midnight and discovered a woman was sleeping at his feet.

"And it came to pass at midnight, that the man was startled, and turned himself; and, behold, a woman lay at his feet. And he said, Who art thou? And she answered, I am Ruth, thine handmaid. Spread, therefore, thy skirt over thine handmaid; for thou art a near kinsman. And he said, Blessed be thou of the Lord, my daughter: for thou hast shown more kindness in the latter end than at the beginning, inasmuch as thou followedst not young men, whether poor or rich. And now, my daughter, fear not; I will do to thee all that thou requirest; for all the city of my people doth know that thou art a virtuous woman. And now it is true that I am thy near kinsman; howbeit, there is a kinsman nearer than I.

Tarry this night, and it shall be in the morning, that if he will perform unto thee the part of a kinsman, well; let him do the kinsman's part. But if he will not do the part of a kinsman to thee, then will I do the part of a kinsman to thee, as the Lord liveth. Lie down until the morning.

"And she lay at his feet until the morning; and she rose up before one could recognize another. And he said, Let it not be known that a woman came into the floor. Also he said, Bring the cloak that thou hast upon thee, and hold it out. And when she held it, he measured six measures of barley, and laid it on her; and she went into the city. And when she came to her mother-in-law, she said, How hast thou fared, my daughter? And she told her all that the man had done to her. And she said, These six measures of barley gave he to me; for he said to me, Go not empty unto thy mother-in-law. Then said she, Sit still, my daughter, until thou know how the matter will fall; for the man will not be in rest, until he have finished the thing this day" (Ruth 3:8-18).

What Ruth did that night, she did by faith, trusting in the grace of God. Boaz responded to Ruth by grace, because grace always responds to faith just as love always responds to submission. What Boaz did for Ruth illustrates what our Lord does for us when we submit to Him.

He Accepts You

Boaz responded to Ruth in three ways. When you yield yourself to the Lord and put yourself at His feet, these are the responses that you can expect. First, *He accepts you.* Ruth was an outsider who had absolutely no claim to the promises that God had given to Israel, for the Moabites were not allowed to enter the congregation of Israel. Ephesians 2:11,12 explains the plight of all Gentiles: "Wherefore, remember that ye, being in time past Gentiles in the flesh, . . . that at that time ye were without Christ, being aliens from the commonwealth of Israel, and strangers from the covenants of promise, having no hope, and without God in the world."

Ruth is a picture of every unbeliever. She was a despised Moabite who had no claim to the covenants and promises that God had given to Israel. She had no hope, but still she trusted the God of Israel: "Thy people shall be my people, and thy God, my God" (Ruth 1:16).

Boaz had commended Ruth for her faith when he said to her, "The Lord recompense thy work, and a full reward be given thee by the Lord God of Israel, under whose wings thou art come to trust" (2:12). The phrase "under whose wings" does not refer to the wings of a mother hen. It refers to the wings of the cherubim in the tabernacle. In Psalm 36:7,8 we read: "How excellent is thy loving-kindness, O God! Therefore, the children of men put their trust under the shadow of thy wings. They shall be abundantly satisfied with the fatness of thy house." Psalm 61:4 says, "I will abide in thy tabernacle forever; I will trust in the shelter of thy wings." Where were those wings? They were in the Holy of Holies in the tabernacle. The wings of the cherubim overshadowed the mercy seat. When Ruth put her faith in the living God, she entered the Holy of Holies and was accepted by the God of Israel.

It's interesting to note that when Ruth said, "Spread, therefore, thy skirt over [me]" (Ruth 3:9), she was actually saying to Boaz, "Spread, therefore, thy *wings* over me." It is the same word that was translated "wings" in 2:12. In other words, if Boaz put the corner of his cloak over Ruth, it would be his way of saying, "I accept you."

Boaz not only accepted Ruth, but he also blessed her. "Blessed be thou of the Lord, my daughter" (3:10). When you trust Jesus Christ as your Saviour, He accepts you and blesses you. You are no longer a stranger, living without hope and without God.

Some people find it difficult to believe that Christ could really accept them, and they live in bondage to their past. But Christ does not accept you on the basis of your own merit, works or character; so by faith, *accept your acceptance!* Notice in verse 9 that Ruth did not say, "I am Ruth, the Moabitess." She simply said, "I am Ruth." She had put her past behind her and forgotten it. Don't be shackled to what you once were, what you did or what people said about you. Don't let the experiences of the past hinder your present life. The Lord Jesus Christ accepts you, so believe it by faith.

He Assures You

Boaz responded in a second way to Ruth. He not only accepted her, but he assured her: "And now,

77

my daughter, fear not" (Ruth 3:11). Just as Boaz assured Ruth, so *Christ assures you.* When you yield yourself to Christ and grow in your relationship to Him, you will not be afraid, for love casts out fear (see I John 4:18).

Boaz also assured Ruth that he would keep his promises and meet her needs: "I will do to thee all that thou requirest" (Ruth 3:11). How do we know that we don't have to be afraid? Because we have the promises of God's Word. His Word assures us that He will do what He has promised and that He will meet our needs.

The Lord sometimes works *for* us, sometimes *in* us and sometimes *through* us to solve our problems. Ruth could not solve her problem, nor could Naomi. Boaz was really the only one who could solve it. God helps us solve some problems for ourselves. Sometimes He brings other people into our lives to help us. But there are some problems only He can solve.

Boaz told Ruth, "Don't go back to Naomi empty-handed" (see v. 17). I think he was being a little humorous here because he knew that Naomi had complained about coming home empty. Word had circulated that Naomi was bitter because her hands were empty. I think Boaz smiled a little when he said, "Go not empty unto thy mother-in-law" (v. 17). However, the significance of this action was that Boaz was giving Ruth a down payment on all of the wealth she would inherit. He was implying, "Don't worry about a thing because I am going to meet all your needs!"

He Assists You

When you submit to the Lord Jesus, He accepts you, He assures you and *He assists you*. In Ruth 2, Ruth was working for Naomi. She had been gleaning in the field, but now the situation has changed—Boaz starts to work on Ruth's behalf.

Our Boaz is also working on our behalf. He finished the work of salvation on the cross, and now He is interceding for us in heaven. He is building our lives, working in and through us. He is also preparing a home for us in heaven in anticipation of the wedding that will take place when He returns and takes us home.

While Boaz was working for Ruth, Naomi assured her, "Sit still, my daughter, until thou know how the matter will fall; for the man will not be in rest, until he have finished the thing this day" (3:18). The Lord Jesus finishes whatever He starts. "Being confident of this very thing, that he who hath begun a good work in you will perform [complete] it until the day of Jesus Christ" (Phil. 1:6).

Boaz faithfully kept his word to Ruth. As soon as it was daylight, he went to the city gate and waited for the other kinsman to arrive. Then he began the proceedings to redeem the property and to redeem Ruth.

In Ruth 1, Naomi gave Ruth some bad counsel; but in chapter 3 she gave her some very good advice: "Sit still, my daughter" (v. 18). When God is working for you, the best thing you can do is sit still and wait. "Be still, and know that I am God" (Ps.

46:10). I think we often hinder God and make the situation worse by our fretting. We get impatient and upset and try to help God do something that only He can do. God then has to remind us to wait. When He is working, we do not need to worry.

When the sun came up, it was the dawn of a new day for Ruth. She had come home with a ten-day supply of grain! She began her new life in Bethlehem as a gleaner who picked up the leftovers in the field. Then the reapers gave her handfuls on purpose. But now the lord of the harvest has given her about two bushels of grain! He was saying to her, "Don't be afraid. I have accepted you. You can be assured that I am now going to assist you."

In Ruth 1, Ruth and Naomi reaped what *they* had sown, and it brought trouble. But now they are reaping what *Boaz* has sown and are experiencing great blessings. We are all involved in the harvest, but do we want to reap what *we* have sown or what *Christ* has prepared for us?

Don't be afraid to put yourself at the feet of the Lord Jesus Christ. He is the Lord of the Harvest. He is the One who has all the resources necessary to put your life back together again. He will accept you and forgive your sins. His Word assures you that you have nothing to fear because He will assist you by meeting all of your needs. The present and the future are under His control, so we can relax and trust Him.

Chapter 10

What Does a Wedding Cost?
(Ruth 4:1-10)

You and I do not own anything because God owns everything. We just use what He gives us. When we act as if we are the owners, we begin to worship our possessions, which is *idolatry*. When we understand that we are only the users of the possessions God has entrusted to our care, then we understand the principle of *stewardship*. This principle also applied to the people of Israel. God owned their land and assigned it to the various tribes and families. The land had to stay within that tribe and within that family. If a family became poor and had to sell their land, the property would revert back to them in the Year of Jubilee or a wealthy relative could redeem the land for them. This was the law of the kinsman-redeemer, which we must understand when we read Ruth 4.

"Then went Boaz up to the gate, and sat down there, and, behold, the kinsman of whom Boaz spoke came by, unto whom he said, Ho, such an one! Turn aside, sit down here. And he turned aside, and sat down. And he took ten men of the elders of the city, and said, Sit ye down here. And they sat down. And he said unto the kinsman, Naomi, who is come again out of the country of Moab, selleth a plot of land, which was our brother Elimelech's; and I thought to tell thee, saying, Buy it before the inhabitants, and before the elders of my people. If thou wilt redeem it, redeem it; but if thou wilt not redeem it, then tell me, that I may know; for there is none to redeem it beside thee, and I am after thee. And he said, I will redeem it. Then said Boaz, What day thou buyest the field of the hand of Naomi, thou must buy it also of Ruth, the Moabitess, the wife of the dead, to raise up the name of the dead upon his inheritance.

"And the kinsman said, I cannot redeem it for myself, lest I mar mine own inheritance. Redeem thou my right for thyself; for I cannot redeem it. Now this was the manner in former times in Israel concerning redeeming and concerning changing, to confirm all things: a man took off his shoe, and gave it to his neighbor; and this was a testimony in Israel. Therefore, the kinsman said unto Boaz, Buy it for thyself. So he drew off his shoe. And Boaz said unto the elders, and unto all the people, Ye are witnesses this day, that I have bought all that was Elimelech's, and all that was Chilion's and Mahlon's, of the hand of Naomi. Moreover Ruth, the Moabitess, the wife of Mahlon, have I purchased to be my wife, to raise up the name of the dead upon his inheritance, that the name of the dead be not cut off from among his brethren, and from the gate of his place. Ye are witnesses this day" (vv. 1-10).

One word repeated many times here is the word "redeem." We need to understand three aspects of the law of the kinsman-redeemer, which picture our redemption in Jesus Christ.

The Characteristics of the Redeemer

The first aspect of redemption we want to examine is *the characteristics of the redeemer*. According to the Law, not everyone could be a redeemer. To begin with, the redeemer had to be *a near kinsman* (see Lev. 25:25). If a poor Israelite had to sell himself into slavery or had to sell his property, a kinsman could redeem the person or his property. But the redeemer had to be a *near* kinsman. He could not be simply a distant relative or a concerned friend.

For Jesus Christ to redeem us, He had to become our near kinsman. "Forasmuch, then, as the children are partakers of flesh and blood, he also himself likewise took part of the same, that through death he might destroy him that had the power of death, that is, the devil, and deliver them who, through fear of death, were all their lifetime subject to bondage" (Heb. 2:14,15). Our Lord became a man, because only in His humanity could He become our near kinsman and pay the price to redeem us. In order to conquer the Devil, who had the power of death, it was necessary for Him to die and be raised to life, thus breaking the yoke of bondage forever and delivering us from death, debt and fear.

83

A second characteristic of the kinsman-redeemer was that he had to be *able to redeem*. The kinsman needed to have enough money to redeem the person or property and to care for it once it was his. Ruth could not redeem Naomi, and Naomi could not redeem Ruth. The redeemer was required to have freedom as well as finances. A person in bondage could not redeem another person in bondage. Boaz was a wealthy man and therefore was able to be the redeemer.

Boaz is a beautiful illustration of Jesus Christ, our Kinsman-Redeemer. Our Lord is extremely rich in grace, mercy and kindness. He possessed all the wealth of heaven, and yet He became poor to make us rich. Only Jesus Christ had the ability to redeem the whole world out of its bondage to sin.

Boaz went to the gate of the city and sat down. He then invited the other kinsman and the elders to sit down with him. In fact, five times in Ruth 4:1-10 you find the words "sit down." Boaz sat down to begin the work of redemption, but Jesus sat down when He had finished His work of redemption. The price was paid once and for all (see Heb. 10:10-12).

In addition to being a near kinsman and being able to redeem, the kinsman-redeemer had to be *willing to redeem*. Boaz presented the offer of redeeming the land to the nearest kinsman as required by the Law (see Lev. 25:25), but in doing so he combined it with the law concerning marrying the widow of a dead brother (see Deut. 25:5-10). Boaz told the kinsman, "When you buy the land, you also must buy Ruth and marry her."

The other kinsman was willing to redeem the land, but he was not willing to redeem Ruth. Why? He was afraid he would jeopardize his own inheritance if he spent his money redeeming another man's wife and land and raising children in the dead man's name. He said, "I must preserve my own name." Boaz was not concerned about preserving his name or wealth. His only concern was doing the will of God and rescuing Ruth. Because the other kinsman sought to preserve his name and inheritance, his name has been lost to history forever. Boaz was willing to redeem Ruth, and as a result, his name will be remembered for eternity!

The Lord Jesus is also willing to redeem. God is merciful, gracious and kind. He does not want anyone to perish (see II Pet. 3:9). He bore our sins on the cross because He wants to save us. Jesus Christ not only purchased our inheritance for us, but He made us part of His inheritance. We have the opportunity for redemption because Christ, our Near Kinsman, has the power to save us and is willing to redeem whoever comes to Him in submission.

The Cost of Redemption

The second aspect we will examine is *the cost of the redemption*. A price had to be paid. Boaz could not go to the gate and say, "Let's all be very gracious and loving. We'll just forgive all past debts and give Naomi and Ruth a new beginning." No, he knew that the only way to redeem Naomi and Ruth was to obey the Law.

God does not save us on the basis of His love but on the basis of His grace. Grace is love that is willing to pay a price. God was willing to obey His own Law and pay the price that the Law demanded. What was the price? "The wages of sin is death" (Rom. 6:23). "The soul that sinneth, it shall die" (Ezek. 18:4). God's Son fulfilled the requirements of the Law by dying in our place: "In whom we have redemption through his blood" (Eph. 1:7). Peter recognized that we were not redeemed from our empty life-style by corruptible items, such as silver or gold, but we were redeemed by the "precious blood of Christ, as of a lamb without blemish and without spot" (I Pet. 1:19). And this redemption is eternal (see Heb. 9:12).

As far as we know, all of the plans Boaz made were made privately. We have no record that he spoke to Naomi about buying the property. The city did not know that Boaz and Ruth had met at the threshing floor. But while the plans were made privately, the price was paid publicly.

This is also true of our salvation. All of the plans for our redemption were made before the world was created. Jesus Christ is "the Lamb slain from [before] the foundation of the world" (Rev. 13:8). But the price was paid publicly when Christ was nailed to the cross.

The Consequences of Redemption

The final aspect of redemption we need to consider is *its consequences*. Ruth's life and Naomi's life were put back together again! The past was forgiven, for all of their debts were paid. The present was assured because they were no longer enslaved. (Boaz actually bought Ruth to be his slave; but because he loved her, Ruth knew she would not be treated as a slave.) The future of the two women was insured because they now had an inheritance in Boaz and his wealth. They knew he would take care of them.

By the time we reach Ruth 4, we see that many wonderful changes have taken place. Ruth has gone from loneliness to love, from labor to rest, from emptiness to wealth, from bondage to freedom, from worry to peace, from disgrace to glory, from fear to assurance and from despair to hope.

What made all of this possible? *Someone paid a price.* Even though salvation is free, it is not cheap. The price of our sin was very costly for our Lord. We dare not underestimate how great the agony of bearing the sins of the world and being separated from His Father was for the Lord Jesus. Someone had to pay a price, and Christ did it willingly.

Some people say, "Since God is a loving God, He will forgive me apart from any sacrifice." No, a price must be paid. Suppose someone steals your car, drives carelessly and wrecks it. The police find the wreckage and then find the person who committed the crime. What would you do if you came to the courtroom and the judge said, "Well, this person is really not too bad. I think we will just let him go"? You would say, "Now wait just a minute, Judge! Someone has to pay for this. I have to buy a new car. Who is going to pay for it?"

The same principle applies to our redemption. We have sinned and are guilty before God. We are obligated to pay the price for our sin, which is death. Just like Ruth and Naomi, we are in bondage and are bankrupt slaves. We cannot free ourselves; someone must pay the bill for us. Who will do it? Only the Lord Jesus is able and willing to pay the price.

> There was no other good enough
> To pay the price of sin;
> He only could unlock the gate
> Of heav'n and let us in.

Have you accepted by faith the redemption that Jesus Christ purchased for you?

> Lifted up was He to die,
> "It is finished," was His cry;
> Now in heav'n exalted high:
> Hallelujah, what a Savior!

What does a wedding cost? For Boaz, it was not cheap because he had to redeem Ruth as well as the land of Elimelech. But because of his love for Ruth, he was willing to pay the price. The cost of redeeming His Bride, the Church, was also very great for Christ. But because He loves us, He also was willing to pay the price. Christ "loved the church, and gave himself for it, . . . that he might present it to himself a glorious church, not having spot, or wrinkle, or any such thing; but that it should be holy and without blemish" (Eph. 5:25,27). Even though Christ has purchased our redemption and made it possible for us to be set free from sin's slavery, we must accept what He has done on our behalf. Until we accept Christ's redemption, we will not be able to put our life together.

Chapter 11

Here Comes the Bride!
(Ruth 4:9-22)

Everyone likes a story with a happy ending, and the Book of Ruth is that kind of story. The book began with three funerals and three widows weeping. But the book ends with a wedding and, ultimately, the joyful birth of a baby boy. At the beginning of the Book of Ruth, everything is falling apart; but at the end, life has been put back together again. If this story were a work of fiction, someone might say, "But life isn't that way. People don't always live happily ever after." That's right; but the Book of Ruth *is* true, and these events happened to *real* people. Everything ended "happily ever after" because the people obeyed God.

The Lord can put your life back together again if you will give all the pieces to Him. Then, instead of being a burden, you will become a blessing. Instead of having a life that is falling apart or that is causing others to fall apart, you will be rejoicing and will encourage others. But the first step toward becoming a blessing to others is to yield yourself to Christ and obey His will.

A Blessing to Boaz

In Ruth 4:9,10 we see the first of five ways in which Ruth was a blessing. *She was a blessing to Boaz.* "And Boaz said unto the elders, and unto all the people, Ye are witnesses this day, that I have bought all that was Elimelech's, and all that was Chilion's and Mahlon's, of the hand of Naomi. Moreover Ruth, the Moabitess, the wife of Mahlon, have I purchased to be my wife, to raise up the name of the dead upon his inheritance, that the name of the dead be not cut off from among his brethren, and from the gate of his place. Ye are witnesses this day."

It's interesting to note how the relationship between Ruth and Boaz changed. In chapter one Ruth did not even know Boaz. Being a Moabitess, Ruth was a stranger to everything that belonged to Israel—the covenants, the promises, the hope, the blessings and the people. Ruth and Boaz were strangers in chapter one. In chapter two they became acquaintances. Ruth realized that she was gleaning in the fields of Boaz. She saw how gracious and kind he was to her. She looked on him as her benefactor until she discovered he was a kinsman. In chapter three she put herself at his feet, and he received her and promised to marry her. The benefactor became a potential bridegroom. In chapter four Boaz redeemed Ruth and married her. They were committed to each other for life. God used Ruth to be a blessing to Boaz.

Boaz loved Ruth and wanted her to be his wife.

91

He was gracious, good, generous and kind to her. He poured out all of his love on her. The only way Ruth could share in the blessings God had given to the nation of Israel was to marry someone like Boaz. *He paid the price.* She literally became his slave, but she was not afraid because she knew how much he loved her.

Ruth was a blessing to her kinsman-redeemer. Have you ever stopped to think that you and I should be a blessing to the Lord Jesus Christ, our Kinsman-Redeemer? We are a part of His Bride, and we should bring joy to His heart. This may be a new thought to you. You might have prayed today, "Lord, help me to be a blessing to my family, to the people at church, to those I work with, to everyone I meet." But have you ever said, "Lord, I want to be a blessing to You"? Can the Lord look down on you and me and say, "Here is my beloved child in whom I am well pleased"? Try to live today so that you will bring joy to Christ.

A Blessing to Bethlehem

Not only was Ruth a blessing to one man, Boaz, but she was also a blessing to an entire village. Ruth 4:11,12 tells us that *Ruth was a blessing to the town of Bethlehem:* "And all the people who were in the gate, and the elders, said, We are witnesses. The Lord make the woman who is come into thine house like Rachel and like Leah, which two did build the house of Israel, and do thou worthily in Ephrathah, and be famous in Bethlehem; and let thy house be like the house of Perez, whom Tamar bore unto Judah, of the seed which the Lord shall give thee of this young woman."

When Naomi returned to Bethlehem with Ruth, she did not bring much blessing with her. She was bitter and complained against the Lord. She was not the best neighbor or the most joyful friend. But now Naomi and Ruth have had their lives put back together again, and the village is saying, "The Lord bless you!"

The crowd that had gathered at the gate gave Ruth and Boaz two blessings. First, they asked the Lord to allow Ruth to be fruitful and build a family just as Rachel and Leah, the mothers of the tribes of Israel, had done. In the beginning of the Book of Ruth, the house of Naomi and Ruth was torn down. Their husbands had died, and they were left childless. In the eastern world, the biggest disgrace a woman could experience was to be barren and have her house remain empty. A woman's only claim to fame lay in her family and their accomplishments. Through Boaz, Ruth and Naomi were given the opportunity of building a new house.

Second, the people asked the Lord to make Boaz and Ruth famous in Bethlehem. The Lord heard their cry and did make Ruth famous, not only in Bethlehem but around the world. In blessing Ruth, the Lord also blessed Bethlehem and made it famous as well. Through the lineage of Ruth, King David was born; and through David, Christ came into the world. Bethlehem not only became the "city of David" but became the birthplace of our Lord. We would not remember Bethlehem today were it not for Ruth. She brought great glory to the city and a living hope to the world.

A Blessing to Naomi

Ruth also became a blessing to Naomi, as Naomi's emptiness was changed into fruitfulness. "So Boaz took Ruth, and she was his wife; and when he went in unto her, the Lord gave her conception, and she bore a son. And the women said unto Naomi, Blessed be the Lord, who hath not left thee this day without a kinsman, that his name may be famous in Israel. And he shall be unto thee a restorer of thy life, and a nourisher of thine old age; for thy daughter-in-law, who loveth thee, who is better to thee than seven sons, hath given him birth. And Naomi took the child, and laid him in her bosom, and became nurse unto him" (Ruth 4:13-16).

Ruth loved Naomi very much. She was loyal to Naomi and lived to serve her. Now that Ruth was married, she could be an even greater blessing to Naomi. She bore a grandson to Naomi who would carry on the name of this family in Bethlehem. To the Jew, maintaining the family name was of utmost importance. When Naomi came back to Bethlehem, she complained because her hands were empty. But now her arms were full with the beautiful life that would establish not only her house but the nation of Israel and, ultimately, the kingdom of God.

Naomi's empty life had been restored and nourished. Because of the blessing of Ruth, Naomi now had a full heart, a full home and full arms and hands.

94

She was thrilled at what God had done. We see quite a change take place in Naomi's attitude from chapter one to chapter four. What made the difference? Ruth placed herself at the feet of Boaz, the lord of the harvest, who willingly redeemed her. As a result, Naomi's life was changed.

A Blessing to Israel

Ruth was a blessing to Boaz, to Bethlehem and to Naomi. *She was also a blessing to the whole nation of Israel.* The Book of Ruth ends with a genealogy (see 4:17-22). Ruth's son, Obed, was the grandfather of David, the highly revered king of Israel. God chose David to establish the kingdom of Israel after the downfall of Saul, and all succeeding kings were to come from the line of David. It was David who wrote many of the psalms. David also made the preparations for building the temple. He received the plans from the Lord and gathered many of the materials needed for the project. He organized the priests, wrote the temple songs and even manufactured some of the musical instruments. David was not allowed to do the actual construction, but his son Solomon completed the temple. King David brought the nation of Israel together and made it strong and great. But his greatest blessing to Israel was that God chose the family of David to be the ancestors of the Messiah, the Saviour of the people of Israel and of the entire world. So Ruth, the Moabitess, gave us the Messiah and became a blessing to the whole nation of Israel.

A Blessing to the World

Because of Ruth's obedience and submission, *she became a blessing to the whole world.* We are still receiving help today from the life of Ruth. She has been, and continues to be, a blessing to the world. She reminds me of Mary of Bethany (see John 12). Mary came to the feet of the Lord Jesus and poured out her love and devotion to Him. She anointed his feet with very expensive ointment, and the disciples criticized her. Judas, of course, wanted the money it could have brought if it had been sold. But Jesus rebuked the disciples. He said, "Leave her alone. What she has done will be spoken of throughout the whole world" (see Mark 14:6,9). When Ruth lay down at the feet of the lord of the harvest, she had no idea that her name and testimony would be spread throughout the whole world, but it has been. And it will continue to be honored until our Lord returns.

Ruth's testimony and example are a blessing to all of us. But, most of all, she is a blessing to the world because she is an ancestor of the Lord Jesus Christ, who is the Saviour of the world.

God can put your life together again. No matter how great your trials are, no matter how much difficulty you may have caused yourself, your life can still be filled with glory and blessing if you will do God's will.

God does not always give happy endings *in this world.* Sometimes we question why God allows certain things to happen. But when the child of God is living in the will of God, he does not have to be afraid of the providence of God. God will accomplish His purposes in a beautiful way.

Do you want to be a blessing to people today? Do you really want to build people up and encourage them? Do you also want to bring joy to the Lord? Then put yourself at Christ's feet and let Him have His way in your life.

Chapter 12

Let's Put Your Life Together!

In this chapter I want to review the entire Book of Ruth and look at three basic lessons that all of us need to learn and practice. If you and I will learn these lessons, God will put our lives together and make us a blessing to other people.

The Book of Ruth can certainly be appreciated on several different levels. From a literary point of view, it is one of the most beautiful biographies ever written. The famous British author and literary critic, Samuel Johnson, once read the Book of Ruth to a group of distinguished men without telling them what its source was. They thought it was a new literary work and praised it highly. Then Johnson told them that the story had come from the Bible, a book some of those men rejected! But we want to approach the Book of Ruth from a *spiritual* point of view and learn valuable lessons from it.

Salvation

The whole Bible proclaims the message of salvation, but in the Book of Ruth we have a beautiful illustration of *what it really means to be saved.* In chapter one Ruth was a stranger from the country of Moab; and as Deuteronomy 23:3 tells us, no Ammonite or Moabite was to enter the congregation of the Lord even to their tenth generation. That sounds pretty final, doesn't it? Ruth was a stranger to all of the blessings God had given to Israel. Ephesians 2:12 is a good description of Ruth and all unbelievers: "That at that time ye were without Christ, being aliens from the commonwealth of Israel, and strangers from the covenants of promise, having no hope, and without God in the world."

Everyone in Bethlehem admired Ruth for what she had done for Naomi (see Ruth 3:11). She had a good character and a fine reputation. She loved her mother-in-law dearly and made many sacrifices for her. Ruth was a humble, hard-working person, but her lovely character could not compensate for her lowly birth. She was born a Moabitess, outside of the family of Israel. Even though she came to the town of Bethlehem and mingled with the Jewish people, she was still a Moabitess.

In a similar way, no amount of good character, fine reputation, sacrifice or hard work can compensate for our birth. We are all born with sinful natures, and we confirm the fact that we are sinners by the sinful acts we commit. "All have sinned, and come short of the glory of God" (Rom. 3:23). We cannot enter the family of God unless we have a new birth. As Christ told Nicodemus, "Ye must be born again" (John 3:7). All of our good works are nothing but filthy rags in God's sight (see Isa. 64:6). Even though we may spend time with Christians and may even be able to walk and talk like a believer, we cannot enter the family of God without a new birth.

In Ruth 2, Boaz came to Ruth. She did not go out to find Boaz; he came to her. What a beautiful picture this is of the Lord, our Kinsman-Redeemer! Boaz was willing and able to redeem Ruth because of his love and grace (see vv. 10,13). He encouraged her with material blessings by inviting her to share his table and by telling his reapers to purposely drop handfuls of grain for her so that she could gather more. Boaz came to her and loved her, just as Christ came to us and loved us, even when we were sinners (see Rom. 5:8).

Ruth went to Boaz and placed herself at his feet in Ruth 3. Salvation not only involves God's coming to us; it also involves our going to Him. "All that the Father giveth me shall come to me [divine sovereignty]; and him that cometh to me I will in no wise cast out [human responsibility]" (John 6:37). I don't understand everything involved, but it is still true. I believe that God chose us in Christ before the foundation of the world (see Eph. 1:4); but I also believe that whosoever will can come and be accepted. This is a mystery we don't understand, but it is a blessing that we can enjoy.

In the fourth chapter of Ruth, Boaz purchased Ruth and took her to be his wife. He lovingly paid the price to set her free. Her inheritance was assured because of what Boaz did for her. Our Lord has also paid the price to redeem us. When we place our faith in His finished work, we become part of His Bride, the Church. Our inheritance is also assured because of what Christ has done. We even have the Holy Spirit as a down payment, just as Ruth received a down payment of grain from Boaz. "Ye were sealed with that Holy Spirit of promise, who is the earnest of our inheritance until the redemption of the purchased possession, unto the praise of his glory" (Eph. 1:13,14).

Ruth's name is found in the genealogy of the Lord Jesus Christ. You find part of that genealogy at the end of the Book of Ruth. Tamar is mentioned in Ruth 4:12, and she was not a godly woman. But she gave birth to Perez (Pharez), who was an ancestor of Naomi. Boaz and Ruth brought Obed into the world; and eventually David was born, and through him Jesus came into the world. If you want your name in the family of God, you must do what Ruth did—yield yourself to the Lord and trust Him.

The first lesson we learn from the Book of Ruth is how to be saved. If you want to put your life together, you have to begin with salvation, with trusting Christ as your Saviour.

Submission

Second, the Book of Ruth contains a beautiful lesson on *submission*. In chapter one we find Ruth *weeping*. Orpah and Naomi are also weeping because they are reaping the harvest they sowed, a harvest of sorrow. "Whatever a man soweth, that shall he also reap" (Gal. 6:7). Naomi and Elimelech had disobeyed God and thereby had sown these seeds of destruction.

In Ruth 1 everything is falling apart. But in chapter two we find Ruth *working*. She is living on left-overs, picking up the grain the reapers are dropping. Ruth is *waiting* in chapter three. Naomi says to her, "Sit still, my daughter" (v. 18). Ruth has submitted herself to Boaz and now is trusting him to work everything out. In chapter four Ruth is *wedding*. She not only has the gifts, but she has the giver—Boaz. She belongs to the lord of the harvest!

We see several examples of Ruth's submission. In chapter two she submitted to Naomi and to those who were in charge of the harvest. In chapter three she submitted to Boaz. In chapter four she becomes a blessing to others because of her submission! Submission always leads to satisfaction. God puts our lives together one step at a time. We first have to be saved, and then we have to submit.

Service

The third lesson in the Book of Ruth is a very important one. It's a lesson in *service*. I believe that Ruth is a beautiful example of what we ought to be as we serve the Lord. If you want to put your life together, you must be a servant. You might want other people to serve you, but that will tear your life apart. If you want your life to change, you will have to start serving others and thinking of them rather than yourself.

The setting for much of the Book of Ruth is a harvest field. Jesus said, "The field is the world" (Matt. 13:38). We are living in the midst of a harvest field, and Christ is the Lord of the Harvest.

102

Did you notice that when Boaz came into the field, he said to the reapers, "The Lord be with you" (Ruth 2:4). They answered him, "The Lord bless thee" (v. 4). That is an unusual way for a boss to talk to his employees. I wonder how many offices or factories have this kind of relationship between employer and employee? What a wonderful master the Lord Jesus Christ is! He wants to bless us. We should never complain about our Master because we are serving the One who paid the full price for our salvation. We are serving the One who loves us, who says, "Let's drop handfuls of blessing on purpose for that person."

In chapter two we find Ruth working *because she had to*. If she had not gone out and gleaned, she and Naomi would have starved. She was living on leftovers. I'm afraid that many of us are living on leftovers. We know that our Master loves us, but somehow we haven't developed a deep relationship with Him. Yes, we are in the field working, but we are somewhat like the elder brother in Luke 15. We are complaining about it. We need to develop the intimate relationship with our Lord that Ruth developed with Boaz.

In chapter four Ruth and Boaz became one. They united their life and love. Ruth was united with all that Boaz possessed. She became a part of all that he was and all that he had. When we realize that we are one with Jesus Christ, that we are not simply laborers in His field but are His Bride, a part of His very life, then our service ceases to be toil and becomes a joy. Our work for Him is then a labor of love. We realize that everything belongs to us because we belong to the Lord of the Harvest.

What is your ministry? Each of us should have a field of service. Ruth said to Naomi, "Let me now go to the field" (2:2). Have you ever said that? Have you found your field? Boaz said to Ruth, "Let thine eyes be on the field" (v. 9). He wanted her to stay in his field and not stray to another one. Don't start looking at another person's field. The grass is always greener somewhere else! We may think other pastors have easier churches, other teachers have easier classes and other missionaries have easier assignments. No, they don't! You should say to the Lord, "Let me go to the field of Your choice. Guide me to where You want me to serve." Then when you find that field, keep your eyes on it. Work together with the other laborers in that field, as Ruth did; and God will bless you richly.

The greatest joy in your Christian life comes when you labor in love for Him, not because you *have* to but because you *want* to. Your purpose for serving is not to receive a reward at the end of the day but to grow closer in your relationship with the Master. When your eyes are focused on the One you are serving and not on the service, then any task you are asked to do is seen as an opportunity instead of a burden. Some people may argue, "But I don't have the skills needed to do this job!" Remember, the Lord of the Harvest loves you. He will not ask you to perform any task that He has not first equipped you to do. "We are laborers together with God" (I Cor. 3:9). The Lord of the Harvest has not asked you to go into the field alone. He is working next to you. Because you are a laborer *together* with Him, He is working *in* you, *for* you and *through* you.

If you want to put your life back together again, the key is your relationship to the Lord Jesus Christ. You will never find true peace or happiness until you turn the broken pieces of your life over to Him. When you try to put your own life together, the pieces will never fall into place.

Where are you in your relationship with the Lord? The first step in building this relationship begins with *salvation*. Christ is your Kinsman-Redeemer. He came to earth as a man so He could die for you. He purchased you with His own precious blood. Have you trusted Him and accepted His redemption?

Your relationship with the Lord does not end once He has redeemed you. You must deepen your relationship in order to grow as a Christian. If you try to control your own life, you will fail. You must place yourself at the feet of the Lord of the Harvest in total *submission* and allow Him to work in your behalf. When you allow yourself to be controlled by the Master, your life will be blessed and He will make you a blessing to others.

Submission must be followed by *service*. Are you busy in the harvest field? Are you serving the Lord grudgingly or gladly? The most miserable people I know are those who are serving themselves rather than God. May we all be like Ruth, serving willingly

105

and joyfully because of our great love for the Lord of the Harvest!

Is your life falling apart because of your sin and stubborn rebellion? Don't run away from your problems, cover up your disobedience or become bitter against God. Christ can put your life back together again if you will let Him. Accept His salvation, submit yourself to His divine will, and serve Him with all your heart; then your empty life will be filled to overflowing with lasting satisfaction.